Too Blessed to be Stressed

How to Find Joy While Raising Small Children

Gaye Burch

Cover Design: Laura Lundy
Cover Picture: Carlisle Blackwelder
Layout: Brenda Kay Coulter, Laura Lundy
Editor: Janet Crews, Linda Gunter Phillips
Printed in the United States of America

Acknowledgments

I could not have finished this book without my editor Janet Crews. Although I have never met her in person, we have become wonderful friends. Her expertise in the editing world and her eye for detail are much appreciated.

Thank you to my writer's group: Brenda Hill, Gretchen Horton, Shannon Steuerwald, and Madeline Gornell for being honest and supporting me in my writing.

A special thanks to Brenda Hill who is responsible for starting our writers' group. Brenda made sure I didn't give up, and encouraged me to keep on the road until I published my book.

My husband probably would have let me sell the house if he thought it would help me accomplish my dreams. His support is priceless.

Thank you, Hugh Lasater, for the beautiful and meaningful poem at the end of my book.

To my children:
Drew, Carlisle, Gentry, Owen, Isabel, Kenna, and Molly.
The greatest gift I have ever been given, apart from my salvation in
Jesus Christ, is the blessing of having all of you. Although I am far
from the perfect mother, I am the perfect mother for you. God gave
you to me and allowed me to be your mother. What a blessing!

To my husband:
I could not imagine being a mother without you.

To my parents:
Your example of steadfastness through the hardships of parenting
means more to me than you know. Your love is constant and sure, and
I am realizing more and more how extremely fortunate I have been to
have you as my parents.

Contents

Prologue

Driving the hour to the hospital in the middle of the night was all too familiar. Because I hadn't been so lucky in the past, I was desperately praying that my midwife would be the one on call this weekend. Why did my babies always come in the middle of the night and on the weekends?

Over thirty years ago, during the summer following my high school graduation, I took a trip with my mom from South Carolina to Minnesota. I had spent several of my growing-up years in Minnesota, and we were going back to visit some very good friends. On that visit, I was intrigued with a family we met who lived way out in the middle of nowhere and had twelve children. One of the sons of this family had just recently married my good friend.

My friend and her husband lived in a small log cabin on his parents' property. As we were shown around the property, we also went into his parents' house. The kitchen was alive with aproned girls, steaming pots, glass jars, and the counters and floor were covered with tomato slop. I was fascinated! Salvaging what they could from cases of tomatoes donated to them from a local grocery store, the sisters—young and old—were canning tomatoes. I vividly remember one of the little girls was diligently working from a step stool. It was intriguing to me, the city girl that I was.

After spending some time in the kitchen, we walked farther out on the property and watched as the men of varying ages worked in the family's sawmill. Most likely during this part of the day I was more intrigued with the good looking young lumberjacks than the actual mechanics of the sawmill.

Being single and wanting to marry one day, I continued to stare at the jeans and boots. (Every day as I was growing up, I watched my father leave the house for work dressed in a suit and tie. To my knowledge, my father has never owned a pair of blue jeans.) That day I was watching handsome men earn a living by the sweat of their brows. Seeing brothers and sisters working hard together introduced me to a whole new world.

It was then and there I decided more than anything I wanted to be married and have a lot of kids.

Be careful what you wish for!

Eight years later at the age of twenty-six, I was married to a man who walks out the door every day for work in blue jeans and work boots. Before our fifth anniversary, I had a three-year-old, a two-year-old, a one-year-old, and a baby. And the pregnancy test I was holding in my hand said "positive." I remember sobbing in the shower and making plans to hide my pregnancy for as long as I could. Because I was already overweight, I thought I could lose my excess pounds and replace them with the increasing baby weight, and no one would know. I wanted to share our secret with someone—but with whom? Only a few of my family members and friends would accept with joy the news of baby number five. The responses from casual friends and even strangers were predictable:

- "Don't you know what causes that?"
- "Did you plan this one?"
- "Wow! How many are you going to have?"
- "You know, they make things to prevent that."
- "Can you afford more children?"
- "Don't you think you should give your body a break?"
- "How are you going to put them through college?"

I also received nonverbal responses from some people: a dropped jaw, a gasp, a deadpan look, a fake look of joy, a sorrowful moan, or the worst of all—a look of disgust.

By seventeen weeks, most people knew that my growing girth was not from donuts and ice cream. I couldn't hide it for as long as I thought, and by the time I had "come to grips with it," I looked forward to this new little life growing in me. However, God had a different plan for me, and I miscarried. Off to the hospital again in the middle of the night.

Although many sorrowful memories are connected to my miscarriage, I am not going to write about them now. I did heal from that somber experience, and God did bless us with three more beautiful, healthy children, making a total of seven.

To a lot of people, raising seven children seems like a daunting task, yet I have many close friends with more children than I. No, we don't wear jean jumpers, live in a commune, and bake bread all day. We are normal women with normal lives… even though things get a bit crazy at times.

When my husband and I were planning our wedding, we asked the assistant pastor of our church, a mentor and close friend to my husband, to officiate our wedding ceremony. Before we took our vows, our pastor wanted us to meet for marriage counseling. He bought us each a Bible-based workbook, and once a week we met with him to discuss marriage. Under most circumstances this counseling would seem very normal; in this case, however, it was not. Why? Because our friend, our pastor had never been married. He had been a bachelor his entire life. Who was he to give marriage counseling if he had never been married? Was he qualified? Yes, he was *very* qualified.

The workbook gave us helpful information, but what was even more helpful to me were the tidbits of wisdom our pastor had gleaned through his many years of observing good marriages and not-so-good marriages. He told us what seemed to work well in successful marriages and what didn't seem to work so well in others. We are celebrating our twenty-sixth anniversary this year—we must have learned something!

Just like the tidbits of wisdom from our pastor, my desire for writing this book is to pass along the "tidbits" that have helped me as a parent: biblical truths, observation, reading books, and just good ol' hands-on parenting.

Does raising seven children qualify me to write a book on parenting? I do not feel like I have all of the answers. Neither do I feel like I raised perfect children, but being a mom of seven and a foster mom of six, I am often asked what I would do in certain parenting situations. Many times throughout my motherhood and marriage, people have said to me, "You should write a book."

I am glad I took their advice, and I hope you, my readers, find encouragement and help on these pages.

Before I begin, however, know I am a professing follower of Jesus Christ and accept His eternal salvation. Apart from my relationship with Him, my parenting has no purpose. Of this I am not ashamed. The fundamental elements of Scripture convince me that the Bible is the ultimate parenting guide book, and God is the ultimate parent.

I do believe we are selfish, sinful creatures, and are bent on pleasing ourselves first. This being true, children want to rule themselves, fulfill their selfish desires, and get their own way... as do adults. As soon as we realize these selfish desires need to be undone in a loving, consistent, biblical way, we will be raising kind, obedient, loving children. These children will grow up to impact their world in extraordinary ways.

Some mothers can hardly wait until their children are grown and out of the house. They feel when that happens, they will finally be able to relax and think mostly of themselves and their needs. I beg to differ. Although most of our children are now adults, we are still guiding them through the early stages of making life-changing decisions. We continue to help them as they learn the adult world of finances, job choices, spouse choices, location choices, and try to steer them in the right direction. I am realizing that "parenting" never ends.

Chapter 1

Teach Good Behavior

From infancy, a baby's brain is engaged, and learning has begun. Our child's character is being developed all day long, every day, and most often without our awareness. It is crucial that we are aware of what is influencing the development of this character and what is making him or her the adult he/she will one day be.

I recently went to a memorial service, and, like always, was interested in what people were saying about the deceased. I wondered if I were the deceased, what would people say about me? What adjectives would they use? Would any of them be a fruit of the spirit? Thinking about this usually makes me determined to make a few changes and try harder to be a better person. What words do you think would be used to describe you?

Better yet, take a moment and think about what words would be used to describe your child.

If you asked someone who knows your child well to write down four adjectives best describing him/her, what words do you think he would use? Be honest. Do the words describe good character?

What words do you wish he would write?

Is your child:

- Selfless or selfish: Does your child think mostly of others or herself?

- Kind or mean: Is your child gentle, sharing, and loving... or does he show aggression with hitting and biting?

- Industrious or lazy: Does your child help with work and pick up after herself... or does she leave a messy trail behind her?

- Honest or deceitful: Is your child truthful... or does he lie and leave out parts of the truth?

- Frugal or spender: Is your child learning the value of money... or is she begging to buy at every opportunity?

- Quiet or loud: Is your child often using a normal voice, whispering requests, and laughing... or is he yelling, crying, screaming, belching and singing at the top of his lungs?

- Patient or impatient: Does your child wait quietly and make requests in a mannerly fashion... or does she interrupt often and demand immediate attention?

Think about an adult you would like your child to emulate. What character traits does that person possess? Does this adult possess kindness, generosity, diligence, love, honesty, leadership, frugality, quietness, patience, steadfastness, and humility?

Don't we all want our children to have some, if not most, of these qualities? Don't we all wish these qualities were evident in our own lives?

Good character does not happen overnight. It must be continually taught.

Parenting today is quite different than parenting twenty years ago. I have been teaching children in various classes for over twenty years, and I am definitely seeing a trend toward parents' obsessing over the safety and health of their children instead of caring what kind of people their children are becoming. I have heard of parents spending hours researching the safest car seat available or introducing organic foods to eliminate possible allergies for their children, yet they spend only seconds teaching them what will truly save their lives—godly character.

What kind of adult will your child become?

In order for our children to become adults with good character, we must immerse them in a way-of-life which fosters and encourages godly character traits. We must engage their brains continually to foster "good" actions.

We are training our children 24/7 whether we like to admit it or not. You might say you are training your children only part of the time because they are in school, at daycare, or away from you a portion of the week. Many parents assume what their children learn, observe and are taught is uncontrollable in their absence. Is this true? Who makes the decision regarding how much time they are away from you and under the influence of others? Can we only control our children when they are with us? What daily input *can* you control?

Maybe control is too strong a word. How about the words *influence* or *direct*? Can you influence or direct your child towards good and away from evil? Can you influence toward positive and away from that which is harmful?

The answer is yes! You are the parent for that very reason. You hold the reins when they are with you and many times when they are not. Don't ever think that someone else is responsible for training, directing, and influencing your children. I understand there are times when a parent does not have control over his or her children, but parents underestimate how much influence they actually have. God would not have instructed us to raise godly children if it was impossible.

Fortunately, in America today, we can still direct our children's lives. Parents are being brainwashed, however, into *managing* bad behavior instead of *teaching* good behavior. The benefits and joy of a well-trained child versus an undisciplined child is a thousand-fold, but it takes dedication, determination and lots of time.

Our family loves to go to Disneyland. Entering the park is absolutely breathtaking! The decorations, music, buildings, rides, cleanliness, landscapes, uniforms, and parking are magnificently controlled by design. It is obvious to any patron the park is a well-organized "ship," and without control it would be disastrous. With over 16,000,000 people entering the gates every year, Disneyland is still a successful fairyland. How does this happen?

Disneyland management trains their staff to control all areas of operation. This training does not happen overnight but is done diligently. Policies, regulations, instructions, and expectations are all included in this training.

Employees do not know ahead of time what positions they will be given. They are hired and then told where in the park they will be working.

At Disneyland, I enjoy seeing the uniforms directly related to the "land or ride" area in which the employees are working. Some of these uniforms (more like costumes) can be quite humiliating or comical. When I was younger, I felt sorry for the young guys who had to wear knee highs and knickers. In all my years of going to Disneyland, however, I have never seen a uniform sloppily-worn, a hat askew, a shirt untucked, underwear showing, or stained clothing.

God would not have instructed us to raise godly children if it was impossible.

Although Disneyland is generally extremely crowded, and standing in long lines is inevitable, I cannot recall ever hearing an employee complain. Nor do I remember ever seeing an employee frown, use a cell phone, or be distracted by another employee. They are well-trained and well-controlled; therefore, they are pleasant workers who exemplify good character.

Somewhere along the line, parents have let go of the training and parenting of their children and given it to others: government, school teachers, friends, and media. Most of all, parents have given the reins of their authority back to their own children. With God's help, parents need to take it back.

The following chapters break down some of the ways in which children are usurping their parents' authority and basically raising themselves. I will point out ways in which a child is "in charge" of certain situations, and then, using biblical principles, I will present some ways in which parents can train their children to understand what good character and God-appointed authority is.

Chapter 2

Your Child *Is* Imitating—But What?

Children are great imitators and act out what is in the world around them. Parents these days love to blame their children's bad behavior on something or someone else, for they don't want any of the blame to fall on them. The blame might be a grandparent, caregiver, teacher or the children's ages. The biggest blame these days is a diagnosis, such as ADD. You might think at this point I am going to say to keep the blame on yourself as the parent. I will get to that, but the number one blame is what your child sees and hears day in and day out.

> Beloved, do not imitate what is evil, but what is good. Anyone who does what is good is from God. Anyone who does what is evil has not seen God (3 John 1:11).

I can remember my mother saying, "You've been hanging around _____too much. That's exactly what she would have done."

Sometimes a parent will say, "You must have gotten that habit from _____. I never taught you to act like that."

What did your children hear yesterday? Whether or not you think they heard or *understood*, what did they hear?

Kids imitate what they hear, such as:

- What were the words to the music they heard?
- What did they hear on the TV?
- What did they hear you listening to on social media?
- What movie were you watching they could hear?
- What did they hear you say in your phone conversations?
- What did you say in the front seat of the car you don't think they were paying any attention to?

Who knows what they are hearing when they are not with you! The Child Development Institute states children by the age of two understand two thousand words.

Children imitate everything!

I have always enjoyed watching my own children get creative and play out a film they had recently watched, a book they had just read, or a person they had just spent time with. If the movie or book was set in medieval times, I would hear my children referring to each other as "My Lord" or "My Lady." If it was "Little House on the Prairie" they had just been watching, someone would be designated as mean Nellie, and the kids were quite good at imitating the syrupy sweetness of Mrs. Ingall's voice. Light sabers were swung through the air if Star Wars was the movie of the day, and oftentimes after watching a romance, the kids might be down the hallway performing a wedding.

Not only do children imitate fiction stories, but they also imitate what is happening in the real world. They imitate fathers, mothers, pastors, priests, teachers, librarians, cashiers, dancers, policemen, fire fighters, restaurant servers, and whomever they see on a day-to-day basis.

When I was little, my brothers put on a tie, carried a briefcase and pretended to go to work just like our dad. When my own children were little, they imitated my husband's going to work by wearing work boots, strapping a knife to their belts, and carrying a water jug. Reading about Daniel Boone or Native American Indians often inspired my boys to wear coonskin hats and carry homemade bows and arrows, or to take their shirts off and paint their faces.

Children imitate everything!

When I had a newborn baby, my girls would carry their baby dolls around with a diaper bag over their shoulders. If I was nursing, they pretended to nurse. If I was bottle feeding, they would feed their babies a bottle.

Sometimes special singing groups would come to our church to perform. For the next few days our kids would sing around the house with a pretend microphone.

Play-acting with children does not have to be taught; it is a natural instinct and a result of what children are exposed to in their daily lives. We all know this to be common and true among children, so why are we not more careful what we expose our children to?

Not too long ago my niece sent me a video of her children. Her four-year-old was playing with her little three-year-old sister. Both of the girls were donned in a medieval-era dresses and were busy playing. The three-year-old was busy singing a made-up song when her older sister informed her they were not going to play *zoo*, but they were going to the Renaissance festival—and off they went.

Where do you think my niece had just taken her girls? You guessed it—to the Renaissance Festival. Where do you think they had been the week before? Yes, the zoo!

After I showed this video to one of my own daughters, I was reminded of the three-year-old girl that used to live next door to us. One day she was playing make believe. She had a purse over her shoulder, bright red lips, sunglasses, and a phone to her ear as she walked out from our tree fort.

My daughter called out, "Emily, where are you going?"

Emily replied without batting an eye, "AA."

Emily's mother was a recovering alcoholic and attended Alcoholics Anonymous (AA) meetings twice a week. Emily had no idea what it was, but she knew it was somewhere her mommy often went, and she wanted to go there too.

Likewise, for ten years I sold jewelry. During these years, I went out to do a jewelry show twice a week. Usually, whatever pieces of jewelry I was personally wearing tended to sell quickly during the show, so I made sure to layer my necklaces and bracelets, modeling as many pieces of jewelry as possible.

Dressed up, wearing jewelry, painted nails, and a bit more makeup than usual is how my children saw me leave the house twice a week. My girls frequently pretended they were going to a jewelry show, and they didn't miss a beat… they would pile on necklaces, bracelets, earrings, and lipstick and walk out the door._

What is surrounding your children? What are they hearing every day? What pictures are on your walls? What are they watching? What or whom do you see them imitating?

The Bible tells us to be imitators of Christ. "Therefore, be imitators of God, even as beloved children…" (Ephesians 5:1 NASB). Paul also said, "Be imitators of me, as I am of Christ" (1 Corinthians 11:1 ESV).

It is crucial we learn Christ's characteristics so we know what to imitate. What good things are your children hearing daily about Christ? Have they ever watched a movie depicting Jesus's life, or a film set in Bible times? Do you have enough story books lying around your house depicting godly character?

Please do not deceive yourself into thinking just because your children are not seeing and hearing negative things, they will be fine. You must immerse them and surround them with positive things.

A small child has no control over what he watches, who he is with, or what he sees. You, as the parent, are in control. It is up to you to make sure the world he is seeing is worth imitating. It will not take him long to become what he has been imitating.

Last weekend we went to the graduation of our friends' twin sons. During the graduation, the graduates and their family members played four beautiful musical selections. The caliber of what we heard was on a professional level, and this was not by chance. It is because the children were immersed in music all of their lives. Not only is music (specifically chosen) played constantly in their home and in the car, but great sacrifices of money and time are also made so that the children can take lessons from accomplished musicians. It is no wonder the twins' youngest sister is now skillfully playing the violin at age eight. She has been immersed in a music world and has been imitating it all of her life.

Evaluating and discerning what is worth putting in our family's lives and finding good things for our children to imitate is sacrificial, and that is okay.

It might mean:

> … you don't watch a certain show anymore

> … you will have to find good music

> … you have to preview a movie or show

> … your child has to sacrifice a friendship

> … you have to sacrifice a friendship

> … your child cannot participate in a particular activity for a while

The list goes on, but whatever is taken away needs to be replaced with something good. There are good films and shows being made, but it takes time and research to find them. There are thousands or possibly millions of good songs available free on the Internet. Positive people are everywhere. Find the positive influences your child needs.

I would like to say that involving your kids in sports is beneficial in many ways, but involvement can be detrimental if the sport means more to you than the well-being of your child. Perhaps an entire chapter should be spent on this topic, but instead I will say this—do not join a sport if you are not willing to drop out because of a harmful influence on your child. I am not talking about physical harm or dropping out because you think the coach made a bad call, didn't let your child play enough, favored his own child with the scoring plays, etc., but rather negative training to your child's detriment. Of course, as kids get older, negative things that are a part of most sports, i.e. bad attitudes, crazy parents, mean kids, and obsessive coaches, make for good discussions and help to train your children how to deal with life in general. Some situations, however, are not worth the negative effect they might have on your child. Always be evaluating to see if something in which your child is participating is worth it.

Your child might not be involved in sports, but might, however, be regularly hanging out with kids in the neighborhood. We are to be kind to our neighbors, hospitable, and even help them if they are in need—no matter what they act like; but spending hours at a time in someone else's home might not be the wisest way for your child to spend his time.

My kids learned a jingle at summer camp: "You are learning habits from your friends every day; you better walk, walk, walk with the wise."

You are making the choices concerning what surrounds their lives. Be willing to make changes and sacrifices. Children imitate! Surround them with something worthy of imitation.

Chapter 3

Keeping a Diary

Keeping a diary might not sound like a help for raising children with godly character, but in my book, anything we can do as moms to make the training of our children easier is important enough to merit a few pages in a diary or some other kind of book.

I am now fifty-two-years-old and my memory is slipping (at least that is what I am told). The other day I was playing a game with my family and some friends. This game requires a member on each team to give clues. Each clue giver spends quite a while figuring out the best one-word clue to give to his teammates. I was the clue giver on my team, and I had just finished giving many clues. When the game was over, someone asked if we were going to play another round. I quickly piped up and said, "Yeah! Let's play one more round. I really want to give the clues."

After a two-second delay, my thirteen-year-old looked at me, made a quick assumption, and realized that I was not kidding. I think she had a hint of sympathy... just a flicker, and then she said, "Mom, you just gave the clues."

I really couldn't believe it, and it hit me hard. *I am losing my precious memory.*

I cannot tell you how many times I have wished I had kept a diary during my early parenting years. I wish I had written just a few pages in a notebook every month so I would have more memories and facts to refer to. I started the notebook habit late, but I benefit from everything I write. Keeping several different notebooks at one time makes my parenting facts flow with more organization.

First of all, at the top of each page, I write a date and a couple of words to give me a quick indication of what is written on that page. This helps later when I am looking for something specific from years earlier. Keeping separate notebooks for different topics can be extremely helpful as well. Specify on the outside of each notebook what the subject matter is and maybe the time frame in which you filled that particular notebook.

Following is a list of suggested notebook titles:

Sickness: I have been asked so many times over the years about certain illnesses, rashes, prescriptions, diagnoses, doctors' visits, doctors' names, hospital visits, and home remedies I used, and it is unfortunate that I do not have more notes written down for reference. Oh, how helpful that would have been all these years if I had created those references. Jotting down a sentence or just a few words is all that is needed for easy referral in the future. Don't worry about format and flow, just write something down. Logging the name of child, age, sickness, symptoms, fever, dates, doctors' visits, medications, etc., can be helpful later.

You may find similarities in sicknesses or some helpful remedy you used long ago that you have forgotten. Having references to the past will help whisk away worries and fears because you can see how you got through it before. It is also helpful to see if a certain child is getting sick at the same time of year, or the same time of the month. Sometimes you may think a sickness is happening constantly, when in fact, a year may have passed and you just thought it was constant.

Holidays: Simply logging where you went, what you ate, and who was there are not only fun facts to look back upon but are also helpful when you are getting older and all holidays seem to run together. Jotting down simple details also helps when your children tell you that you have done a certain thing every year, when in fact you have done it only twice. Money spent, cards sent, food prepared, and gifts given are a few of the things to jot down in your holiday notebook.

Children's Schedules: Over the years, many young mothers have asked me how I scheduled feedings, naps, meals, activities, and sleep. Even if you are not a firm believer in schedules, referring to what age a certain child was when they did certain things is of great use. Remembering type and amount of food and formula, bedtimes, sleep patterns, etc., is extremely helpful for moms with gaps between children, babysitters, grandparents, and foster moms.

Extracurricular Activities: : Include what lessons they took, at what ages, and also from whom. How much did it cost, etc.

Births and Deaths: Each year designate one page for births and one page for deaths. You will open this notebook more than you think.

Yearly Highlights: Graduations, weddings, birthdays, parties, guest lists, out-of-town guests, vacations, world news events, new things bought for the house, house repairs, and other important things are always fun to look back on and very helpful when written in a concise way. Don't forget to write family member's milestones, i.e. learning to swim, walk, ride a bike, getting a driver's license, graduation, winning an award, new jobs, breaking a bone, getting braces on or off—to name just a few.

I have often thought it would be fun to have notebooks on the living room table with different titles, and anyone could write in them. Just think about how much fun and how useful that would be to read again and again, not to mention some things I don't remember will be remembered by someone else.

Maybe by the time you read this I will have five notebooks filled to the brim on my coffee table.

Chapter 4

Teach Your Children Compassion

Our children are born selfish. Their thoughts are on no one but themselves from the minute they are born. This thought process does not have to be taught; it comes naturally. A baby has no idea if his demanding cry for milk is at a convenient time or not. He simply demands you think of him at that moment and of no one else.

This selfish behavior can either be undone through consistent teaching and influence, or it will, on its own, become a selfishness affecting your children the rest of their lives.

Teaching your children to think about others and not of themselves starts at a young age. They are learning through everything they hear and everything they see. Examine your own life and determine if your children are seeing selfish, stingy behavior or generous, giving behavior. Your behavior does not go unnoticed. Your behavior is what they are learning. Because I homeschool my children, I am with my kids all day. It is very daunting at times to know my behavior has such a huge influence on my kids.

The Bible clearly teaches compassion, specifically through the life of Jesus. "Seeing the people, He felt compassion for them, because they were distressed and dispirited like sheep without a shepherd" (Matthew 9:36 NASB).

My family lives in a small town, in a very low-income area in southern California. Because of the warm climate, many homeless people tend to ask for money on street corners all over our city. Because these homeless people are quite numerous, they are often the topic of conversation in our family. One day I decided I would help these extremely needy people instead of turning my head the other way. I stopped trying to determine how they might spend the small amount of money I was going to give them and just simply give. Judging by outward appearances, I could assume these street-corner "bums" would, most likely, foolishly spend my money on drugs and alcohol.

Should this deter my giving? Are we to judge the receiver before we give?

Not only does my split-second glance of these homeless people tell me that they do not make very many wise choices, but my observation also tells me they are in need of food and clothing. I determined it was more important that I teach my children, by example, to help those in need than to judge what negative outcome my help could possibly have.

This being the case, I started handing money to these homeless people from my car window, simply because the Bible teaches us to help those in need.

Most often, when pulling up to the stop sign, the homeless person is on the passenger side of the car, and it is easier for my kids to hand the money out of their windows. Although this sometimes freaks them out a little bit, depending on the person they are handing money to, this teaches my kids to give to those in need, no matter what they look like, and not to make judgments that are not ours to make. Even little ones in a car seat are observing and thinking about what we are doing… and they continue to mull this over in their little brains, learning all the time.

Not only do we see lots of homeless people, but we also see vagrant travelers. These travelers wait near the freeway on-ramp I use every time I am headed the twenty miles home. (This freeway [40] actually stretches from California to North Carolina, which is why so many people are hitchhiking on this particular one.) Because my car's seats are usually full, and we are overflowing with groceries, we do not tend to give rides to these travelers. It is to my advantage that we are in the car when we see hitchhikers, however, because it leads to some really great conversations that cause my children to think. Car rides are an exceptional time for quiet reflection and good conversations.

My conversation starters, in reference to these homeless, vagrant people, might (depending on the ages of my children) sound something like this…

- I wonder if that man has any children?
- I wonder if that man slept outside last night? … I am so thankful we have comfy beds to sleep in.

- I wonder what he had for breakfast? ... We are so blessed to have breakfast every day.

- I wonder what his friends were like when he was little? ... It is so important that you choose friends who are making good choices.

- Do you think he ever goes to be with family on _____ (name whatever holiday is coming up or has just passed)? I am glad we have a family to spend holidays with.

- Wow! He had to make a lot of bad choices to be standing there on that corner. You make sure that you make good choices, in all you do, so you don't end up on a corner.

- Do you think they wish they were somewhere else? Where do you think they would want to be?

- I wonder if he has tried to get a job?

- I wonder what his hobbies were when he was little?

- Isn't it interesting that God has the number of hairs on his head numbered just like he does yours?

As you get the conversations rolling and their minds thinking, compassion sets in. This compassion will continue to develop and generosity will begin to happen with ease.

However, many times, judgment can stand in the way of compassion. We want to teach our children to be thinking of others in a compassionate way. We want to stir up compassionate thoughts, and we want them to enjoy showing compassion. Jesus said, "Judge not, that you be not judged. For with what judgment you judge, you will be judged; and with the same measure you use, it will be measured back to you" (Matthew 7:1-2).

Our kids do not miss a beat. They hear everything and see attitudes of judgment.

My dad loves to shop. Many times, over the years I have been the recipient of this love through gifts that have included expensive trips, perfumes, and accessories, all of which I never could have afforded on my own. Because of where I live, I used to feel funny wearing or carrying these "high-end" gifts at times. I was afraid I might be perceived as having a lot of money. Perhaps to those who knew I had little, I might be perceived as foolishly spending the little that I had. Being the recipient of such lavish gifts, however, has helped me not to be too quick to judge what someone else is wearing or what kind of purse she is carrying.

I can still remember when I found out a friend of mine was on EBT (food stamps). We were having kids at the same time and spending lots of time together. Not only did she give me an education on food stamps, but one time I recall being in her living room while she was on the phone with the electric company talking about her delinquent bill, begging them not to turn off her electricity. It blew my mind. I had never heard of such a thing (someone's electricity being turned off because they did not pay their bill—why would someone not save enough money to pay their bill?). I was wondering why she was not embarrassed to have the phone conversation in front of me. I would have been humiliated. To her it was part of life.

This same friend told me about WIC, a government program not using food stamps. Although my husband had worked at the same job for fifteen years, we were having babies fast and having a hard time making ends meet. So, I went on WIC. As a Christian, I struggled with whether or not this was right, for we were depending on the government instead of God for our needs. I can still remember being in the grocery store and looking around to make sure nobody I knew was close by before I went through the line. Not only can I remember feeling the heat of embarrassment on my face and ears, thinking the people behind me were passing judgment, but I also remember being choosy about which cashier's line I would go through. (It didn't help that sometimes I was carrying a Coach bag my father purchased.)

It is common in our low income, small town, for the person in front of me in line at the grocery store to be using their food-stamp (EBT) card or WIC vouchers. Some people reading this book might not even be familiar with these forms of payment and would have no idea the EBT card is not an actual credit card. Instead, it is a government food-stamp card. Like the many conversations about homeless people in our town, there are also many adult conversations about the numerous people on "government assistance." These conversations usually include judgment on the items these people put on the conveyor belt to purchase.

"Shame on them for buying filet mignon, real butter, or donuts with our taxpayer money!"

Oh, the conversations of judgment I have heard! These conversations can get really interesting if the hand using this food stamp card has freshly-manicured nails, or if the card was pulled out of a designer handbag. And—*heaven forbid*—she has an expensive cell phone!

Do not be too quick to judge.

- Maybe the food is for an out-of-town guest or a special occasion.

- Maybe their expensive purse or watch was a gift.

- Maybe this is the first time they have ever used assistance, and because of some terrible tragedy, government assistance was their last hope.

- Maybe they have never worked, are lazy, and are always on government help.

- Maybe they have a family member or friend who is paying for their phone, which is not unusual.

Maybe. Maybe. Maybe.

Let God be the judge, not us! Let us put our minds on what God wants us to focus on, training our children to have compassion, which in turn leads to generous giving to the needy.

I know a lady (Louise) who used to volunteer at a homeless shelter for women and children. She became acquainted with a young mother (I will call her Patty) and her three small children. As she got to know Patty, she found out why she was living in this homeless shelter. She did not pass judgment, although from what she found out, judgment could have easily been passed. Instead, she felt compassion and began to reach out to Patty and her children.

Over the years Louise has purchased groceries, appliances, and furniture for Patty. She has also taxied Patty to numerous medical appointments, court dates, DMV appointments, and to work. She has stood by her side during altercations at her children's school, cried with her over the loss of loved ones, been there when Patty's son went to prison and when he got out, listened to her sorrows when her girls got pregnant out of wedlock, and counseled her through harmful relationships. Her children have been the recipients of school supplies, school clothes, birthday gifts, fast food jaunts, and Christmas gifts—all at the generous hand of Louise. Many years into their relationship, Louise even bought Patty a *car!*

Yes, Patty continued to make many foolish decisions in her life, but eventually she was able to move out of the homeless shelter, get a job, rent a home, own a car, and raise her family. The compassion and generosity of one person impacted her in many positive ways. I am sure it did not go unnoticed by her children. Imagine the ripple effect it is having even today!

Maybe you do not have the means to be generous in the way in which Louise was, but everyone has the capability of being generous in some way. Children can learn to be generous by observing our willingness to share with others.

Lending Our Belongings

We can all think of someone we know who is quick to lend their personal belongings to other people. We can also all think of someone to whom we would not want to lend our things. Your children know if you are quick to lend to those in need. Teach them the importance of helping other people. Start this when they are very young. Don't underestimate what your children are learning through observation.

Years ago I had a friend who would ask me if she could borrow some of my baby accessories. Because I was still planning on having more children, I selfishly didn't want to lend to her. I had learned from past experiences of lending to this friend that if my things were returned in one piece, they would need extensive deep cleaning to get them back in the condition in which I had lent them. I did not want to lend to her anymore, *especially* my cherished bassinet. One time when my own baby had just grown out of the bassinet (and my borrowing friend was pregnant), I asked a different, very close friend if I could *give* her my bassinet to store in her garage. Then, if and when my pregnant friend asked to borrow it, I would be able to say that I had given it to someone else. Well? It was true, wasn't it? I had *given* it to my friend to put in her garage. That was okay. Wasn't it?

No! Worrying about the condition of a bassinet and whether it would be returned for my next baby was not worth my children's failing to see the opportunity to help someone in need.

It has taken me a long time to learn that possessions are just temporary, and we are not taking our possessions to heaven with us. Do not become too attached to what this world holds.

Make a choice to be around people who lend and give easily, for these are the kind of people you want your kids to emulate. Remember, children learn by observing.

Allow your children to see your lending and giving. You do not necessarily need to call your kids in from outside just so they can observe your handing an item over to someone. Nor do you need to devote an entire dinner conversation to what you gave away. When kids observe good behavior, they want to copy it. When I see a child sharing with ease, my mind immediately thinks well of the parents because I assume this behavior has been learned through the child's observation of their parents. Do not underestimate how much your child is learning from seeing you lend or give to those in need.

Sometimes your children's lending and giving has a negative or humorous side. Young children do not have enough wisdom to know when to give, what to give, and how much to give. Sometimes kids want to give away things that are not even theirs, which can be embarrassing at times, especially if you have to call a fellow parent and ask for the item back.

Your child might volunteer your time to the leader of an activity while you are standing there. The leader then looks at you with such hope and anticipation for your positive response, only to hear you say how sorry you are you won't be able to help. Or maybe, after your child has volunteered your services, you are too embarrassed to say that you can't, so you end up doing something you dread or do not have time to do.

When you are on your way home or when your guests have gone, talk about what happened. Make sure your children know how great it is that they want to help others, but you would like to plan ahead before something like this happens again. Talk about how some similar situations will "play out" in the future. Do not spend too long on this one offense, but in the near future, bring into conversations with your children principles on giving and lending, so they do not forget what they have been taught.

If you hear of someone in need of children's clothing, tell your children the situation and go with them to their room to pick out some things they can give to the child in need. Assure them they do not have to give away their favorite shirt.

Try not to give their belongings away without their knowledge. Please be respectful of your children's belongings. If they are not ready to give something away, then let them keep it. I love to "clean out," and I remember many times trying to talk my kids into giving away things they wanted to keep. (To my regret, my adult kids have told me I did give away some [they say a lot] of their things they did not want to give away.)

Children do not have a concept of value, and are childish, so they might want to give away everything they own, not to mention give all your things away as well. Some of our kids wanted to give something away every time their friends came over.

A friend brought her child over for a play date, on one occasion, and as they were leaving, I gently pointed out that her child was "accidentally" taking my son's favorite Lego toy. (I thought the child was being sneaky and stealing the toy.) But this little "thief" piped up and informed me that my child had given it to him. How embarrassing! In front of the parent and child, I was on the spot to say something everyone would accept as a good enough reason for getting the toy back. I cannot remember the exact words I used, but I do remember I was extremely embarrassed. (Just for a tidbit of information—twenty years later we are still friends, and I just oohed and aahed over a picture of my friend's grandchildren. The father of these two children is the little "thief.")

The Legos leaving the house was not the issue, and most of the time it would not be a big deal if something was given away. Sometimes, however, the item being given away might be sentimental, or maybe you have numerous children and don't want every toy given away before they are handed down to the rest of your children, or maybe it is one of their sibling's toys they are nonchalantly giving away.

We finally made a family rule: if they wanted to give a friend something, they had to ask permission after he went home. If the answer was yes, they could give it away the next time they were together. This rule was easy to understand, and it accomplished everything we wanted it to—teaching our children that giving was a good thing, but guidelines were necessary.

If a child's mind is geared with thoughts of compassion toward others, his behavior will lean toward generosity and kindness. This kindness will seep into so many areas, even when your child is very young. A young person's mind is constantly in gear, and we want those gears to be well-oiled with biblical principles, such as compassion.

In what way are you training your child to be compassionate?

Chapter 5

Demonstrate How to Serve Others

A person must learn to be a great servant before he can learn to be a great leader. The last chapter talked about developing compassion in your child, which leads to a generous, giving spirit. This chapter talks about raising servants.

"Bear one another's burdens, and thereby fulfill the law of Christ" (Galatians 6:3 NASB). This law of Christ is a life of selfless love.

Serving others takes time, and being generous with your time can be tricky. Finding a proper balance between giving of your time to serve others and saving enough time for your family is a task that takes skill. I have found that an easy way to kill two birds with one stone is to make "serving others" a family activity.

Take your children with you when you are helping. They can be assigned a task within their capabilities. Happily inform your children what you will be doing and how they will be helping you. This help does not need to be optional. They will soon, from a very young age, understand helping is not only fun but also something your family does together. According to the understanding level and the age of your children, explain to them why the person or organization needs your help. Give as many details regarding the situation as possible; these details help your child understand the great need and stirs in them the desire to serve. For instance, if you are preparing a meal for someone who just had surgery, explain to your child—without too many graphic details—what the surgery entails, what that person's limitations are, and how much time is involved in recovery.

I liked to get my children's minds going by saying things like:

- Can you imagine what it would be like not to be able to get up for ten days? I wonder if he misses being outside?

- I wonder if she cried when the doctor was "fixing" her.

- I wonder if he had to get a shot.

- Do you think she has someone picking up groceries for her family?

- I wonder if he has other people helping him? I hope so, because he surely is going to need it.

Occasionally, when opening a jar is difficult, I might say to the kids within earshot, "Wow! I wonder how_____ (I name an elderly person living alone, that my child knows) gets her jars open. I'll bet there are times when she can't get it open, and so she has to find something else to eat."

The goal is to get your children's thinking on the needs of others, which, in turn, takes their minds off of themselves and makes them want to serve the needy.

Even the youngest child can be involved in helping. For instance, a small child can tear the lettuce leaves for a salad when making a meal for someone. When it comes time to deliver the meal, have your children help you carry the meal in from the car. Save carrying the bread for the smallest child.

Help a widow or someone who just had surgery with yard work. Even a little child can pick up piles of debris and pull weeds.

> But whoever has the world's goods, and sees his brother in need and closes his heart against him, how does the love of God abide in him? Little children, let us not love with word or with tongue, but in deed and truth. We will know by this that we are of the truth, and will assure our heart before him (1 John 3:17-19 NASB).

A friend of ours accidentally cut off his right thumb. It was devastating because, unfortunately, he is right-handed. I decided that we should take him dinner, and while fixing his dinner, I was astounded when I realized every task I performed in his food preparation needed a thumb. I wasted no time in bringing this to my children's attention. Emphasizing how wonderfully and intricately we are made by God's design, and how uniquely different the thumb is from the other fingers, I helped the kids to understand the tragedy of the situation. My desire was to develop compassion and a desire to help in their hearts and minds.

Sometimes serving others is as simple as holding a door open for someone. Remember, kids are watching everything you do and are constantly learning. Don't forget to say thank you when a door is being held for you. Remember children are listening as well. Ask them to come up with their own ways they can serve others. Little ones love to come up with ideas and sometimes this can be hilarious.

Be creative and find ways to ingrain this godly characteristic of servanthood into your children's lives. In what ways are they learning to be servants? Who can you serve this week?

Then the King will say to those on his right, "Come, you who are blessed of my Father, inherit the kingdom prepared for you from the foundation of the world. For I was hungry, and you gave me something to eat; I was thirsty, and you gave me something to drink; I was a stranger, and you invited me in; naked, and you clothed me; I was sick, and you visited me; I was in prison, and you came to me." Then the righteous will answer him, "Lord, when did we see You hungry, and feed You, or thirsty, and give You something to drink? And when did we see You a stranger, and invite You in, or naked, and clothe You? And when did we see You sick, or in prison, and come to You?" And the King will answer and say to them, "Truly I say to you, to the extent that you did it to one of the least of these brothers or sisters of Mine, even the least of them, you did it for Me" (Matthew 25:34-46 NASB).

Chapter 6

Comparing Yourself Is Toxic

Comparing yourself to other people most often leads to the sin of jealousy and pride. Be careful! We all like to feel good about ourselves because we are human. Part of feeling good is comparing ourselves to others. If we are better than they are at something, that makes us feel good, and this way of thinking seeps into our parenting. When our children excel in a certain area, we like for the credit to point to us, their parents, which is ultimately pride. If our children are not excelling in a certain area, however, then we look to other parents whose children are exceptional in that particular area and become jealous. Both pride and jealousy are sinful attributes we should avoid. Give gratitude to God for excellence in your children and petition to God for help with your child's weaknesses. Look up to Him for your gauge, not at others.

It is really hard to compare two things that are nothing alike... *so don't* compare yourself to other moms and *don't* compare your children to other children.

Comparing yourself to other parents or your children to other children is futile. The earlier you learn this, the earlier you will rid yourself of hours and hours of discouragement. This world today can be discouraging enough on its own, so don't purposefully add to it by comparing. I wish I had learned this early on as a parent. Although I sometimes still find myself comparing, I have learned how detrimental to parenting this can be.

The three things I hear moms comparing the most are:

> My child can read!
> My child is potty trained!
> My husband is the biggest help!

Although the first tooth, first smile, crawling, walking, formula or breast milk, etc., are often compared, they are not comparisons based on the achievement of the parent but more on each child hitting those milestones on his or her own. Reading, potty training, and husbands, however, are comparisons reflecting more on the mother.

My child is "potty trained" means something different to *everyone*. "Potty trained" to one mom might mean her child went potty more than once without being prompted. Hearing your friend's child is potty trained, and you haven't started training your own child, can be a bit overwhelming. This friend may have neglected to tell you, however, that this "going potty" has only happened a few times; and in fact, her child has daily accidents, wears pull-ups, and still wets the bed at night.

"Potty trained" to another mom might mean her child has been in underpants 24/7 for six months without a single accident.

It is the same phrase, but it can have several different meanings.

Each child has different parents, different diets, different routines, different toilets, and most of all, different *bodies*. Save yourself some worry and heartache and begin to train your child when he is ready, and eventually your child will be potty trained. (Because I have had so many mothers ask me how I potty trained my children, I have included a chapter on potty training in this book.) *Do not compare!*

The same goes for "my child can read"! This means many different things as well. "Reading" to one parent might mean her child can read an entire book. What she may not tell you is she has read that same book every day to her child because it is his favorite; hence, the child can "read" the book because it is memorized. Or perhaps the child can sound out enough words to form sentences, and so the phrase "can read" *is* appropriately used.

Another parent, with a child doing both of these things might not say her child "can read" because he cannot pick up a random book and smoothly read its contents.

Reading is a great accomplishment and of great importance, but not for bragging rights, nor to put another parent to shame. The ability to read is one of the greatest gifts a parent can give to a child. Be earnest about giving him this gift, but *do not* compare.

"My husband is such a great help." This is another thing young moms commonly compare. Face it—some husbands help and some husbands don't. Some husbands help voluntarily; some husbands have to be asked or will help only when nagged. Some husbands cook; some husbands don't. Some husbands will clean up vomit; some husbands won't. Some husbands change dirty diapers; some husbands don't "do" diapers. Comparing your husband with another can ruin a family, and the sooner a wife accepts the fact all husbands are different, the happier her marriage will be and the more joyful she will find her task of mothering.

Last, but not least: do not compare grandparents. They are not the same people, you are not the same daughter, and your kids are not the same grandkids. Houses, locations, vehicles, income, spouses, number and ages of children, etc., all play a huge part in a grandparent's involvement. Because everything is so different, they cannot be compared. Make your life easy and tell yourself you will be thankful for any help and attention you get, and rest assured many people out there have no grandparents or help at all.

I am not writing all of this to sound uncaring, but rather to encourage you to put on blinders and stop comparing your life to those around you. Look to the Lord instead. Look to His Word to see how you are doing with your parenting. As mothers, we have a lot on our minds, so I encourage you to close the door of comparing yourself to others so that you can experience freedom that only God can give as we look to him.

I cannot finish this chapter without writing this warning. If you are having a spirit of discontentment and find it hard each day to find peace and joy in your present circumstances... get off social media. Take a break from spending hours looking at the lives of others and focus on what God wants for your life. I think we all know the ways in which social media can negatively affect us, and we need to take heed and be warned to look with caution on the lives of others through social media.

Now those who belong to Christ Jesus have crucified the flesh with its passions and desires. If we live by the Spirit, let us also walk by the Spirit. Let us not become boastful, challenging one another, envying one another (Galatians 5:24-26).

Chapter 7

Potty Training

Numerous moms have asked me how I "potty trained" my own children. I was very fortunate with all of my children to be able to count on one hand the total number of times I changed sheets because of night-time accidents. I do believe that my potty training techniques work really well, but I am also a firm believer that much of bedwetting is hereditary.

"Potty trained" means something different to everyone, and sometimes I think conversations started about "potty training" are a way for many parents to brag.

I said that I have many tricks up my sleeve, and someone might be reading this and want some hints before they venture down the "potty training" trail. This is what I did.

1. Wait until your child consistently wakes up with a dry diaper for several weeks before starting.

2. Invest in pullups.

Pullups can be expensive, but they are definitely worth it. I do believe if you start training too young or are inconsistent in training, your children could possibly be in pullups for more than a year. In that case, you are wasting a great deal of money and should not invest in them. If you try my "tricks," in most cases, only a few packages will be needed.

3. Get a "potty training" wardrobe ready.

Use nothing but elastic-waist clothing. Period. Pulling down or pulling up with ease is vital. This is not a time for being cute. You want as few frustrations as possible. Put away the dress-up clothes, batman capes, long sweaters, overalls, onesie pajamas, and especially pants that button or have a difficult snap. Don't make it any harder on yourself or your children than it needs to be.

4. Buy a kitchen timer and "poo poo" treats.

My children very regularly went "big potty" about a half hour after breakfast. Because of this, I would set the timer to go off at the time when I usually changed a stinky diaper. Set the timer, put them on the potty, hand them a book, and stay close by. Take this time to pluck your eyebrows, floss your teeth, clean the sink, apply makeup, etc. The key is not to distract your children by talking to them or cheering them on because this causes their bodies not to relax. Simply set them on the potty and turn away to do your own thing. Your children will enjoy that you are in there with them; and then they can relax, and you will not be hurrying them because you are getting things done as well. Run the water or whistle a tune, and when the timer goes off, this potty session is over.

Even if they didn't go, pick them up off the potty, tell them they did a good job, pull up their pants, and set your timer for one hour later. It will click in their brains, and before you know it, they will hear the timer go off and walk to the bathroom. Still go with them, however, still put them on the potty, and still set the timer. If they did not go the previous hour, more than likely they will go this time. Keep your eyes peeled just in case they want to try again before the next hour. Then if they "go," give them a potty treat. I usually gave tiny treats like an M&M or Mike and Ike. Important: Do not give them a treat for trying. This will defeat the purpose. Do, however, praise them for trying.

5. Put them on the potty at the top of every hour.

The most important thing about this step is I did not discuss with my children whether or not they had to go potty or whether or not they wanted to try again. I went to where they were (even if they were playing nicely, or watching their favorite show), picked them up, and told them and with a happy voice the buzzer went off and it was time to sit on the potty again. If they already went "big" potty for the day, they do not need a book or timer. It is crucial that your children do not think they have a choice in the matter of "potty training."

After each time, set your timer for one hour later. When your timer goes off, simply go get them and set them on the potty. Do not cajole them into wanting to go. Be matter of fact and have a friendliness about you; pull their pants down and manually put them on the potty. Wait. When they are done, wipe them and get them down. At this point you can tell them you are setting the timer for a little while later, so they will know they will be doing this again. Keep your voice chipper. No cajoling or overtalking about it. Just state the facts. (I have to say I was definitely not perfect in the friendly tone always but got better at it as I potty trained more children.)

Why do I put them on the potty? Because it saves time, frustration, and allows the children to understand it is not optional. Before you know it, they will be doing it themselves. This also saves them from having accidents as they try to get their pants down in time. You can avoid all of these simple little accidents by being in charge at the beginning until they get the hang of it. Think of it as teaching a teenager to drive. They have to drive around the block a bit before they get on the freeway.

6. Start at a good age.

I see so many moms starting to potty train when the child is way too young, and therefore, they are potty training or dealing with surprise accidents for more than a year. I also see mom's waiting until the children say they are "ready," but this also brings a lot of inconsistencies because the child has a choice and is not necessarily being trained. They are simply given an available potty and go whenever they want, leading to a longer training period, and many accidents.

I would suggest waiting until they have their second birthday and the weather is warm to even think about starting the training. I waited for the weather because we have a cold house, and I concluded that when the house was warmer, they could relax. The potty training went much better. I usually waited until they were about two and a half to start potty training. Because they were a little bit older, they understood better what was going on, and this usually paid off. We would be accident free 24/7 within approximately two months of the onset of training.

I would figure out when my child was going to be two-and-one half-years-old and then figure accordingly. Sometimes I would start them a little before two-and-a-half and sometimes I would start them a little after. First of all, it depended on when I thought I would have a month of really good weather. Waiting for warm weather also meant that the children had on less clothing, and it made the whole process much easier.

7.   Clear your calendar.

Not only did I want the weather to be right, but I also wanted a fairly empty calendar. If I had several days in a row of being home, this proved to be the best time. Having a lighter load on the calendar helped me be more consistent in potty training. However, even when I was out shopping for the day, I put them on the potty at the top of the hour. This helped prevent many emergency situations of being in a long check-out line with one of my children needing to go potty.

After they were well on their way to going on their own, I would continue to tell them when to go to the bathroom. It was not their choice, and I made sure they followed through with it. Our consistent times for the bathroom were first thing in the morning, mid-morning, right before lunch, before naps, after naps, before dinner, and before bed. I was very aware of the time because it seemed like I was always potty training somebody.

Some moms might think that if you remind a child too much, they will never learn to go on their own. After seven children and years without any accidents, I concluded I would rather make my child go on a regular basis than to clean up accidents and launder sheets day after day. It also takes much less time to remind them to go potty than it does to clean up accidents.

I have had many friends over the years who have had more than one child who is a habitual bed wetter. I think this is a different situation altogether. A habitual nighttime bed wetter is different from a child who consistently uses the toilet and yet is having sporadic accidents for a couple of years. Many children's bladders do not mature in the same manner as other children, and their problem is usually only a nighttime one. For these children, a slowly maturing bladder seems to be a genetic condition. I have learned to neither judge these children nor their parents.

So, clear your calendar, gather elastic-waist clothing, buy a timer, invest in pull-ups, wait until they are old enough, manually put them on the potty with a cheerful voice, and hopefully you will have quick success!

Chapter 8

Stop the Mealtime Nightmares

Who is in charge of mealtime in your home? Are you deciding what your children eat? Or do you ask them what they want—as if you have handed them menus. Are your children deciding what utensils to use—fingers, forks, or spoons? Or do you have some say in the matter?

Are your young children sitting in a chair instead of a highchair because they don't want to be in a highchair anymore? Or do you wish they would sit in the highchair because it would eliminate your having to clean the floor after each meal?

Are you fixing four different menus to appease your toddlers?

Are you throwing food away on a regular basis because they don't want what you have given them or because you have given them way too much?

Do your children determine the actual time of the meal? Or have you decided?

Are you packing five different snacks for the day because you are not sure what your children will eat that day?

Are your children begging, whining, or crying about food?

Things can be different!

Mealtime can be a favorite part of your day because of the break it gives you. Your children will look forward to the food because they are hungry. Your children can sit in their seats and eat what is put before them without whining or complaining.

You can look forward to mealtimes if you learn how to eliminate mealtime frustrations. This allows mealtimes to be a break in your day that you can look forward to. If you are guilty of cajoling your children to take one more bite, finish their food, or constantly battling with them over what they will eat, then getting over this hurdle will simplify your life in an exciting way.

Mealtimes happen hundreds of times throughout the year, so the sooner you make changes, the sooner you will have delightful meal breaks throughout your day.

Before you make any changes, you must have full confidence your children *will not starve* as you implement these new mealtime guidelines in your home.

Here are a few tips I used in our family to make mealtime a joy and a much-anticipated break in the often tiring day.

First of all, when my children seemed to be dilly dallying over their food and did not seem interested in eating it until I was taking their food away from them at the end of the meal, I decided to put into action a meal "time frame." The goal of this was to have my children actually eat during meal times. This does not have to be so rigid that mealtimes are no longer a joy.

Inform your children a change is about to take place. Implement this method until your kids understand that while it is dinner time, it is time to eat. Even very small children understand this.

If your young children do not have a concept of time, then use a simple kitchen buzzer. When the buzzer goes off, the meal is over. Explain this new time frame to them. Make sure they are looking at you when you tell them about the timer and its purpose, and then repeat the new "time" guidelines at the beginning of every meal for about a week. It is also beneficial for your child to repeat to you what you have just said.

Using a timer helps your children have a concept of how long a meal in your home actually is. They will get the hang of this very quickly, and they will actually be eating during the meal. Soon the buzzer will no longer be needed.

Second, put *tiny* amounts of food on their plates—*a tiny amount.* This trick teaches them to look at their plates and not be overwhelmed by large amounts or something they don't like. You might even want to give them a smaller plate.

As they learn to eat tiny amounts of food, you can start to increase the amount. Do not put a lot of what they like, and a small amount of what they do not like; make the amount of each food the same—tiny. We all know children can consume a great deal of macaroni and cheese, chicken nuggets, and many servings of bread, but ask them to eat one mushroom or a small piece of tomato and the gagging reflex begins. Following the *tiny* rule trains them to try new things and to like vegetables as well as junk.

Third, when starting this new eating plan, simply inform them at the beginning of the meal that if they want more of something, they must finish everything on their plates first. Then they may ask for more of whatever they like. They will soon get the hang of eating what is set before them, enjoying your new foods, and knowing that they can have more of their favorites. You will no longer have to cajole them into taking one more bite or talk them into liking a certain item. This frees meal times to be a time of refreshment and sweet conversation.

When they have finished their food within the time frame allotted, they may have dessert. (I didn't serve dessert very often, but that is up to you.) It is important, however, to understand that it is okay for one child to have dessert and another child not to have dessert. They will not die, and they will soon learn to finish their food if they want dessert.

Fourth, and an extremely helpful guideline, when the designated time frame for each meal is over, the meal is finished. This is probably the most important step. For instance, if your child has two peas left on his plate, and the buzzer goes off—the meal is over. It is that simple. It is hard to take the plate away and not allow him to have more of his favorite thing or not allow them to have dessert when he was being such a good boy during the meal, or when he was so close to finishing what was on his plate.

Don't worry! It will be okay! It is simply part of the training process and will not happen often if you are consistent. It can also be emotional if children think they are being punished by not having dessert when they actually haven't done anything wrong. Take heart and do not cave under this emotional pressure. This scenario is vital to eliminating mealtime battles in your future.

When you remove the plate, say in a matter-of-fact, joyful voice, "Good job! You almost finished on time." Then give them immediate encouragement for their next meal. "I think at dinner, you will finish on time and be able to have dessert." (For your own sake, at dinner time, serve them even a tinier amount of each thing. Remember they can ask for more of their favorite things after they have eaten what is on their plates—and of course it is a small amount.) Take courage my friend, your child will not die, and the next meal (training session) will be here before you know it.

If they are consistently not finishing on time, you can try to extend the time a little bit, give a smaller amount, or serve dessert to those who have finished. It will only take one or two nights of their missing ice cream to finish what is put before them in a timely manner. Some parents might think this is cruel. Consistency is so effective in this area. Though occasionally penalized while learning, with consistency your child will not be deprived of dessert because they finished their food. This is not cruelty. You are not running your home in a military fashion. You simply have some guidelines you are implementing to your mealtimes so your meal times are not dreaded but enjoyed. It is loving discipline from you, the God-given person in charge.

The ultimate goal is to have your children sit down at the table, eat what is served to them without drama, and therefore, have joyful mealtimes. Whatever tactics you implement, understand *that they will not have to be implemented for very long if you are consistent.* Keep the plan simple. The simpler it is, the simpler it will be to follow. Children are not confused when the rules are told to them in simple terms, and they will learn to follow the rules if you don't confuse them by changing the guidelines. Be consistent with the guidelines.

The key to this new regime is to be consistent with the simplicity of the guidelines. When they finish what is on their plates, they can have more of their favorites. If they have finished their food on time, they may have dessert.

Try not to talk about their finishing their food during the meal, because you will have already made the rules clear at the beginning of the meal. A couple of reminders during the meal the first few days are okay. The reminders should be simple and said in a jovial, non-threatening way. Show your own excitement by how you give the instructions. Don't underestimate how even a small child can understand, even before they are old enough to repeat the instructions back to you.

Be consistent with the guidelines.

Fifth, don't make false threats, and don't carry one meal into the next. For instance:

"If you don't eat your _____, then you can't have dessert.

"If you don't finish your _____by __(time)__, you can't watch _____."

"If you eat your sandwich, I will buy you something at the store."

"If you eat just one bite, you can have ice cream later."

"You only have two more minutes. Hurry! or you won't be able to have more _____."

Do not bring up past meals!

"You didn't finish your dinner so you can't have _____, or you can't do_____."

It is hard to be consistent if you can't remember what you said from one meal to the next or from one day to the next. That is why it helps if each meal time is separate from the previous eating time. Think of each meal time as a new training session.

Last, have the same menu for everyone. There are some exceptions to this rule, and I understand many times parents will be eating dinner after their young children go to bed, but I encourage you to stick to the same menu for all the children.

I realize some children have allergies. Sticking to a healthy, whole-foods menu will be good for all. If you need to adjust, then by all means adjust. However, the guidelines in this chapter should not be affected by what your children can and cannot eat. Have hope!

It is interesting to note many studies have shown kids outgrow their allergies between the ages of four to six. If your children have allergies, it would be worth your while to have an allergist test your kids every year. Not only do allergies change as kids get older, but so do tastes. Introduce new foods to your kids as they mature.

What your child was once allergic to may no longer be an allergy.[1] Obviously, some adult tastes are not yet appropriate for small children. (In our home I like to pile jalapeños on my plate.) Just remember the goal: for your children to eat what is prepared for them without whining and complaining and to eat in a timely manner.

Now I am about to tell you the number one, key factor that makes this plan work practically without flaws. It is one small word—are you ready?

HUNGER!

Your child will look forward to meals and eating things they have never tried before if they are hungry. We have lost the feeling and benefits of hunger in our fast-food society. We don't know how much fun it is to eat and how much better food tastes unless we are really hungry. I have a feeling that someone might twist this and say how horrible it is to make your children go hungry, and that is not what I am saying at all.

Have conversations with them about hunger, telling them how God made their little bodies to make a noise when it is time for them to eat. Talk about waiting so they can hear the lion roar that

---

1 "In general, as kids get older they can grow out of allergies," says New York-based allergist Clifford W. Bassett, MD, a clinical instructor in the division of infectious diseases and immunology at the New York University School of Medicine, "Don't think that once allergic, always allergic. This is not the case." The largest study of its kind to date, published online in the Annals of Allergy, Asthma and Clinical Immunology in July 2013, found that 3,188 children surveyed currently had a food allergy, while 1,245 had outgrown one. Key findings of this FARE-funded study include:

- A little more than a quarter of the children—26.6%—out grew their allergies, at an average age of 4-5 years old.
- Children who were allergic to milk, egg, or soy were most likely to outgrow their allergies. The likelihood of outgrowing shellfish, tree nut, and peanut allergies was significantly lower.
- The earlier a child's first reaction, the more likely that child was to outgrow the allergy.

God put in their tummies. In order for your kids to hear this roar, they might need to get up, go outside and get some good old-fashioned fresh air and exercise. Kids today, as you well know, spend way too much time inside and in front of a screen. As a result, many kids are having a problem with obesity.

Teach your children about countries where the people are starving to death. Ask them if they think other hungry children would eat anything. Do not use your mealtime to discuss these topics, however, because you do not want it to turn into a tricky way for con-

Hunger is the key for happy mealtimes.

vincing them to eat. Children pick up on trickery, and it might defeat the purpose.

Remember: If your child is hungry, he or she will eat.

Having a couple of small snacks during the day are okay but these need to be in a timely manner. Don't forget to be aware of what they are drinking throughout the day as well. Juice and sugary drinks might be filling them up. Hunger is a major key for happy mealtimes.

Our family loves food. My kids had plenty of snacks, and goodies (candy—maybe too much at times, because I love candy), but overall, they were hungry at mealtimes, and it made for good appetites.

I will throw in a scenario I have seen over and over through the years. Moms describe the food their children are about to eat in hopes they will eat it without a battle. This does not work. Describing the food is putting undue emphasis on the food and causes the child to want to avoid it. A child does not need to know that the green beans they see on their plate are from a can and not from a bag in the freezer. They do not need to know that the texture and color are a little bit different than Mommy's green beans at home. They do not need to know what they are about to eat is good for them. They do not need to discuss the number of beans on their plate. It is exhausting to listen to all of this. Just give them food and let them discover on their own the color, texture, taste and smell of what they eat. If undue attention has not been put on the food, they will probably eat it.

When I was growing up, I remember the anticipation of wondering what was for dinner. The whole family ate the same thing for dinner. Sometimes it was "kid friendly," and sometimes it was not. I remember what I hated and what I liked, but I had to eat both. Yes, I used to try to feed scraps to our dog under the table or put food in my napkin to flush down the toilet later, but I was expected to eat even the things I did not like. We didn't get to whine and fuss at the table, and we were not served a different menu. My mom chose what we ate for meals. That was life, and what a good life it was.

Just five years of eating with your small children adds up to 1825 meals. These 1825 meals can be break times of nourishment, laughter and great conversation; or they can be almost two thousand battles. Changes will not happen overnight, but don't give up. Consistency is worth it in the long run.

When you take back the mealtime reins out of your children's hands and put them back into your own hands, you will have full mouths, joyous smiles, and delightful breaks throughout your day.

It seems too simple, yet so many parents continue meal after meal, day after day, year after year of having hundreds of mealtime battles with their children. Remember you are the parents, and God gave you the authority to train them. If your children are setting the guidelines for meal times, then they are in authority over you.

I will add one more thing—I encourage you to eat with your children for the majority of their meals. They will learn by your example.

I worked at a camp in North Carolina for several summers, and the camp's food was not always the best. Add to camp food hundreds of campers coming in for each meal. Although they received some complaints about the food, before every meal the campers quoted 1 Corinthians 10:31. "So whether you eat or drink, or whatever you do, do it all for the glory of God." This might be a great verse for your family to learn.

Chapter 9

The Benefits of Time Alone

In this world of constant entertainment and action, children are not learning to play by themselves. They are dependent on other people and things to entertain them. A mother used to carry a small toy car or book, or a piece of scratch paper and a pen in her purse, and her children would be entertained and quiet with these things when in public. This is rarely the case in today's society because children are not being trained from the beginning to spend time alone.

When children are quiet and still, they are learning. They are learning by what they hear, and they are learning by what they see around them. When given time with an object, such as a toy, or when given the opportunity to spend time in nature, children learn firsthand about mechanics, texture, taste, smell, and how to be creative. Hence, they are not dependent on anyone else to make them happy or content.

Children's abilities to happily play by themselves for long periods of time is developed by having them learn to be by themselves for short amounts of time. They will increase the time on their own as they learn to enjoy the things around them. Like compassion, time alone develops in your child another Christ-like character trait—self-control.

In one of the classes I regularly teach, I have anywhere from five to ten kids. The children are ages kindergarten through third grade. When I ask the children in my class a question, the ones who have learned self-control answer the questions correctly

Imagine, if you will, eight children ages four to six being asked a question. Several of the children raise their hands before they have even heard the question and answer incorrectly, and some yell out the wrong answer without first raising their hands. Two of the children, sitting still with their hands in their laps, give the question a moment of thought, raise their hands, and wait to be called upon. They are the ones who get the answer right. They have learned patience and self-control.

This patience and self-control does not happen overnight. It must start when they are little. Even a "crazy" two-year-old can learn how to sit in one spot for a long time—maybe to complete an entire puzzle—but it takes training and perseverance on the part of the parent to make this happen.

Although the following verse is speaking about being quiet more than it is speaks of being still, I chose to use it, because when children learn how to be quiet, when the world around them is noisy, they are developing self-control. They are learning how to listen to what they hear, instead of always being the one to make noise. This does not mean that during playpen time your child won't get so enthralled in his or her own little world that you won't hear some noises coming from them.

> The one who has knowledge uses words with restraint, and whoever has understanding is even-tempered. Even fools are thought wise if they keep silent, and discerning if they hold their tongues (Proverbs 17:27-28).

I strongly believe the key to teaching your kids to learn how to entertain themselves and to play happily alone for long periods of time before they are even one-year-old is...

The playpen!

Although playpens are a thing of the past, many of us mothers still believe the playpen is the greatest invention ever made.

Other than conquering mealtime frustrations, playpen time is the number one thing I share with frazzled moms who want a few precious, quiet, uninterrupted moments without a baby-in-arms or toddler underfoot. Playpen time teaches contentment, patience, self-control, and creativity. It was my key to being a happy and sane mother.

This is how I incorporated *"Playpen Time."*

When I use the word *playpen,* I am referring to something like a "Pack-n-Play" you set up in a permanent location and use for your child to play in rather than to sleep in. My friend who runs a daycare just sent me a picture of a play yard which adjusts to the size you want, and she likes it just as much as the "Pack-n-Play." It is now a permanent fixture in one corner of her daycare (along with a Pack-n-Play in another corner). In the picture she sent, the child in the playpen is contentedly playing with the toys around him, while two of the other children are standing outside the playpen wall, looking in—longingly. They have the rest of the room to play in (and every toy you can think of is in this room), but they stand next to the playpen, wishing they could be in it. My friend knows I appreciate the humor in the picture, because we are both such fans of the playpen.

First, set up the Pack-n-Play in a central location. I do not mean in the middle of the room, but neither do I mean tucked away in a bedroom somewhere. Put it where the child can *see* people, because you want your child to learn to play by themselves even when there are others around.

Next, fill the playpen with a variety of toys: something that makes noise, something to chew on, bright things, squishy things, firm things, short toys, longer toys, board books, and whatever else you have lying around that they would like to play with. These toys must only be used for playpen time. I have two sets of toys: one set in the playpen, and the other set stored in a box for a quick and easy playpen toy exchange.

Do not put soft cozy blankets or plush animals in the playpen, because you do not want your child to fall asleep during this time. I started playpen time with my children when they could sit up well, around eight months old. Because you want playpen time to be a time of wakeful play, it is crucial you put them in the playpen when it is *not* time for a nap.

Even though the Pack-n-Play will be in a centrally located room of the house, you want it to be somewhat out of the way... maybe in a corner. You want your child to know he is not alone, but you want to teach him to entertain himself.

This playpen time is such an amazing training time for your children. You will want your family to get behind you in understanding its purposes—patience, self-control, and creativity—along with the bonus of teaching your children to entertain themselves and give you a much-needed break. Ask everyone in the home not to interact with them while they are in the playpen. It is okay to glance at them and smile, but simply walk by. Sometimes for the first week or so, your child may cry when they see someone walk by, or even stand and reach out their arms.

Sometimes they might try to climb out, but they will soon learn to enjoy this personal time. Use a consistent, jovial voice, and set them back down and hand them the distraction of a toy. If you start them with playpen time before they can actually climb out, they will not even try once they are able. Your child learns that you will come and get them before too long. As you start this wonderful journey, you will understand why the following two things are crucial: setting them down and handing them a distraction. If you are consistent, the incorporation of playpen time becomes one of your most crucial tools in raising your children.

All the benefits taught to your child, as well the peace and quiet you get during this time is invaluable.

So how do you start this amazing time?

1. Wait until the child can sit up by himself or herself.

2. Put toys in the playpen (only one set at a time)._

3. Put your child in the playpen. Hand them a toy and use a happy voice. Show them something fun to do with the toy.

4. Walk away but remain in the room.

Some of my kids would immediately engage themselves with the toys, but the second I moved away, they would start to cry. I would very simply lean over, hand them a toy, and say, "No, no," to the crying. Do not be overly concerned about their crying; it is okay for them to cry. Your child is safe and has no reason to cry other than they want to be in charge of where you are. Crying the first few days is natural and can actually be good for them. But every child is different.

I suggest you set a timer near enough for the child to hear the timer go off. The timer is beneficial for both him and you. Be ready to pick up your child the minute the timer goes off. Start with five minutes. Usually, with toys they have never seen, they are willing to sit and play for a while. When you pick up your child, playpen time is over.

Your child is not to go back in there or play with those specific toys—no matter what—until the next playpen time. If he crawls over to the playpen, and from the outside starts to cry for the toys in the pen, then simply say, "No." Do not let him take any of the toys he is playing with out of the pen. He will want to sometimes, but it is simple. *Don't let him.* This is a crucial step, because you want your child to look forward to going in the playpen his next time.

When the timer goes off, get your child out. After they are trained, set a timer only you can hear. This was important for me, because I would be distracted and forget the time. Even if your child is playing nicely, get him out. If he is in there for too long one time, you might decide not to put him in the next time, and so forth. Make it consistent and all will benefit.

I usually did this twice a day. Each week I extended the playpen time by a couple of minutes. The goal is by the time your child is crawling well you will have two thirty-minute periods of time when your child is entertaining themselves without complaining or crying, and you can get some things done. I usually did playpen time right before lunch and right before dinner while I was preparing those meals. Your child will very quickly realize that the time in the playpen is short, that the toys in the playpen are good, and he will enjoy entertaining himself. What is really a joy is when your child starts to babble and sing. I think playpen time was my saving grace when I had a three-year-old, two-year-old, one-year-old and a baby.

I have several friends who did playpen time when their children were young, and we talk about it like it is a lost art of healing. There are very few moms who do this today, and that may be why so many young moms look and talk about being frazzled. Your child will love the time, but it may take increasing your time increments to make it a productive amount of time.

Educating your children at a young age on how to be still and look at things for a long time also benefits other areas in their young lives.

It is really quite humorous when using a timer to see how fast their toys are dropped the minute the time is up. And other times playpen time is so successful, I had to use a buzzer or alarm just for my own sake. Because my children would be so happy and content playing in the playpen, and I would be busy and distracted, I would sometimes forget the time and find them asleep. That wasn't good because then I would miss out on a good nap time in the afternoon. So, a timer was just as important for me as it was for them. All my children got accustomed to this time very quickly and grew to love it. As a matter of fact, sometimes they would scramble to get out of my arms as I leaned down to put them into the playpen, because they would spot a toy they were anxious to play with.

Every week I would change the toys. If you change them too often, your child might not learn how to be creative with what they have. Switching it up, however, brings excitement to the playpen, and the creativity can begin all over again.

Choose to do this at the same time every day. Allow the child to see you and others in the home and to hear all that is going on. This is security for them and teaches them that just because a person is in the room does not mean they have to be the center of attention.

My older children would often practice piano in the same room, and on occasion, the child in the playpen would do a little begging with outstretched arms. On the whole, however, they knew that this was their time to be in the playpen, and they were not getting out until it was time.

I think another important thing is you, the mother, be the one who puts the child in and gets him out. Don't ask me why, but sometimes consistency has side effects we don't even realize. One side effect that I notice when we have playpen time in our house (we still do this with foster children), other people in the house can walk back and forth or be in the same room, and the child in the playpen does not beg to be taken out. They simply do not expect anyone but Mom to take them out. This allows everyone to be able to relax, and only one person has to keep track of the time. But do not forget—after a stretch of consistency, your child will actually be so engrossed in their play they won't be anxious to get out. Playpen time makes for a happy, peaceful home.

Training your child to love his alone time has many advantages. Some of them are: being able to answer an important phone call, being able to go to the bathroom by yourself, being able to cook a meal without somebody hanging on your leg, cooking a meal safely, allowing your older children to create (such as with Legos) without a toddler destroying the creation, and being able to enjoy a quiet conversation.

Playpen time does work. It not only teaches your child to entertain himself or herself, but it also provides a little peaceful "vitamin" to get you through a particular part of each day. Give it a try. Be consistent. Your kids and you will benefit!

Playpen time makes for a happy, peaceful home.

I am adding this way after I have completed my book, but since I am proof reading, this situation fits perfectly into this chapter.

The other day we were invited to a birthday party for a girl turning fifteen. This fifteen-year-old is being raised by her grandmother, and her great grandmother lives with them as well. My two teenage daughters, our sixth month old foster baby and I attended. After plenty of people had held and entertained our baby, it was time for everyone to eat. The two older women wasted no time in getting out a Pack-n-Play, setting it up, and directing someone to put the baby in it. I was delighted! This did not require a discussion. They are both from the playpen era and babysit often. It was obvious to me they are well aware of the benefits of playpen time. Putting our baby in the playpen was practical; she was out of the way, and everyone could enjoy their dinner. Even our baby was happy, although we haven't even started playpen time with her. Everyone could eat their food and enjoy lively conversation without having to distract the baby, feed or entertain her. She was right there safely enjoying her wonderful surroundings.

Chapter 10

Teach Your Child How to Wait

Can your child sit in a chair for five minutes without getting down? Can you instruct your child to sit and wait for you, and after you have left the room for two to three minutes, come back and find him in the same spot?

When I was growing up we had a cocker spaniel named Flair. She was so cute and very trainable. We taught her to sit and stay for very long periods of time. We would make her sit and wait for such long periods of time, it probably was on the border of being cruel, but we were kids and thought it was funny. Our dog's ability to sit and stay did not happen by chance. It took months of working with her every day after school. We literally spent hours training her for this trick.

The same goes for your children. When a child has the ability to sit still because they have been told to do so, they did not acquire this ability overnight. It takes a great deal of practice, and the best time to practice is at home. How wonderful it is to go somewhere knowing your children are able to sit still simply because they have been told to sit still.

Do you find yourself hurrying because your child has not learned to wait? Are you changing your plans because your child is impatient? Has your child trained you to be at his beck and call?

Take a moment, and think about your children's daily lives and how often they must wait. Do they wait for anything? Think about it.

In today's world instant gratification is easy to obtain. Life is fast-paced with electronics in every hand. Not often does a person wait for anything.

I am sitting in my car right now waiting to have a cup of coffee with my friend. Because I am early, I have parked my car in the shade, and I am facing in the direction of a small, slow, four-way stop intersection. I just witnessed a perfect example of a young person who has not learned to wait. I noticed a car had just barely come to a complete stop when the car coming up behind him gave him a toot on the horn. He honked his horn as if to say, "Don't stop for even a second longer than is necessary, because I am behind you." I didn't see the age of the person in the front car, but I did see a very young man in the horn-honking car. This young man did not wait for even one second. He honked his horn to assure that he would not have to wait at all. I wonder what the hurry was. Was he truly in need of that extra second? Did he get an extra second by honking his horn? Would waiting in the normal "four-way-stop fashion" have ruined his day? I wonder. By the way, he never did come to a full stop.

The other day I was in the grocery store, and although I noticed a lot of people on their phones, on this particular day I noticed a child with a large handheld device watching a movie. Seeing a child watching a movie in a public place was not new to me, and at times has merit, but seeing one watching a movie in the grocery store was new.

I think the most interesting fact about this scenario was that we were in Trader Joe's. If they had been in a Super Walmart, the mother could possibly be doing major shopping in all departments, needing to be in the store for a long time. Her child's needing to be pacified with a movie might be understandable. But we were in Trader Joe's! If you are familiar with Trader Joe's stores, you know they are small, so I doubt this mother was going to be shopping for very long.

Could this child simply have walked by his mother's side and looked around? You may be thinking perhaps he was in the middle of the movie already. Exactly! Could he not have waited until he was back in the car to continue watching? Could he not have waited until he returned home to watch it? It was not as though the movie would have continued without him.

It has not always been convenient for kids to have the luxury of taking a movie with them. Kids learn so much just by accompanying their parents on their errands. They are missing out on life when their noses are down.

I realize our world is changing rapidly because of technology, but the importance of children learning to wait for something still exists.

I like to watch old movies and old TV shows. The behavior of children on the shows is always so fascinating. For instance, take Opie on *The Andy Griffith Show*. He is often sitting in the sheriff's station (his dad is the sheriff) quietly watching what is going on around him while he is waiting for his dad. He sometimes had to wait a long time before his dad was finished talking and ready to go. Opie was not acting bored or sitting with a bad attitude—neither did he need to be corrected for touching things around the sheriff's station or be reminded to get back on the chair and wait. He didn't interrupt Andy with pleas to go home. He had been taught how to sit and wait patiently.

We recently watched *The Brady Bunch* on Netflix, and likewise, although the children were not perfect, they were often seen waiting for their parents. Sometimes they were waiting because they were in trouble, and sometimes they were waiting just to have a simple conversation or ask a simple question... but they would sit still and wait.

I loved the *Brady Bunch* when I was little, so I thought my kids would too. I can't say they loved it. It was watched more to make fun than to actually enjoy. However, there are some good things that kids portrayed on the show, as far as respect and obedience, I am glad for my kids to have seen.

One of the interesting differences between today's children and the children in old films and TV is the fact that when the children in older films are waiting, they were usually not doing anything other than watching and listening to what was going on around them. They had nothing in their hands to keep them busy. Although this is not a bad thing, learning to wait without something in your hands is a great skill. Counting tiles on the ceiling and looking at pictures on the wall can be entertainment enough.

I really enjoy watching mealtimes in old BBC series. Even though the families are being served their food, children have to wait because they are served last. Also in these old BBC movies, they practice the old proverb "children should be seen but not heard."

My mom talks about going to the movies as a little girl, and the anticipation of waiting for the movie to begin was part of the excitement. Even now, children get to watch cliff-hanging previews so they do not have to wait for their movie to begin.

I notice many times today parents will get their child's food completely ready and place it on the table before the child goes to sit down; that way they can sit down and start eating right away. Not a moment of waiting does the child have to endure. It used to be a child would sit at the table with his hands in his lap and wait until grace was said; then the serving of food would begin.

Why wait? Waiting is a skill instilling godly characteristics in your child. Waiting teaches patience, self-control, and meekness.

How do you teach a child to wait? Start when they are young and start with just a few things.

Here are a few ways to teach your children patience:

Have them sit at the table with their hands in their laps before you take any food to the table. If they can do this while being quiet, it is even better.

Have them sit in a chair with a book in their lap and teach them to wait for you without opening the book ahead of time. Making them wait for even twenty seconds and gradually increasing to longer amounts of time is excellent training for self-control.

Teach them to stand quietly by your side while you have a conversation. Practice the art of this while you are at home talking to someone else. Be purposeful about finding little ways for them to learn to wait. Start with short periods of time while they are just learning.

Teach them to wait patiently for something they want right now. For instance, buy colorful cupcakes at the grocery store. Build your children's anticipation a couple of days before letting them have one. (Two days may be too long for some children, because they do not know how to wait.) The important thing is that they see the cupcakes and have to wait without eating them right away. When it is time for them to have a cupcake, ask your children to sit down at the table. Let the adults choose first and then serve your children. If your children cannot do this quite easily without yelling out which one they want, or whining for two days about the cupcakes, then you have your work cut out for you. If they succeeded in the "wait," then give them lots of praise for being so patient.

Be creative and find little ways at home to make your children wait. Teaching kids patience at home is easier than trying to teach them in public. They don't need to know that they are waiting or even being taught a lesson, but the more you train them to wait, the more patient they will become.

Because everyone's lives are different, it is hard for me to give examples pertinent for all. Your children can learn to wait in almost every daily situation. Each day is packed with many, many patience-training sessions. Turn life's daily moments into training sessions without your children's knowing. Purposeful training sessions at home result in patient, self-controlled children in public.

As parents, we need to remember why we want our children to be able to have self-control and patience. Why do they need to learn to sit still and wait patiently? It is the picture of Christ! They are fruits of the Spirit. "Put on then, as God's chosen ones, holy and beloved, compassionate hearts, kindness, humility, meekness, and patience" (Colossians 3:12 ESV).

Chapter 11

Scheduling Your Children

Some moms schedule and some moms do not. Because life happens, I am flexible, but overall, when our kids were small, we ate breakfast at the same time, lunch at the same time, dinner at the same time, went to bed at the same time, and naps were at the same time—almost every day. I am a strong believer scheduling makes for happy, healthy children. Children on a schedule eat well, play well, learn well, and sleep well.

I used to ask my own mother about what she had done with us, as far as scheduling, she told me that her pediatrician told me how to schedule our sleeping and eating. He instructed my mom about what was good and healthy for us. Being told by a pediatrician to put your kids on a schedule would probably help most moms, but pediatricians do not instruct in that way anymore. I trust this chapter on scheduling meals and scheduling sleep is helpful.

Just last week our church had Vacation Bible School, and I invited a friend of mine to come over afterwards with her grandchildren to swim. She told me she was babysitting two more children. One of these children had just turned three, so assuming after a crazy, long morning of exhausting activity this child would take a nap, I told her she could bring the kids over after the three–year-old took his nap. She then told me that his mom said, "He didn't take a nap."

What do you think was the reason? It is the same reason I hear over and over from so many moms. If I make them take a nap, they won't sleep at night. This is becoming a pattern with many young moms today. They are following the parenting trends of "their" world, which allows children to mandate what parents can and cannot do. Hence, most children are not taking naps. I have observed these little bodies walking around late in the afternoon cranky, whiny, and full of tantrums. Are children's bodies that different from twenty years ago? Are naps old-fashioned?

In our county (the largest county in the United States), our school district does not "do" kindergarten naps anymore. Half-day kindergarten has long since gone by the wayside. Why is this? I am not sure, but I think it is because many adults have bought into the fact we should not make our kids do something they do not want to do. It is so sad to think about these little children being busy all day long with stimulation and never having an opportunity to rest their little bodies and minds.

Children need naps.[2] It used to be mandatory all over the country for kindergarten children to rest in the middle of the day. No child was worse off because of this rest but instead benefited much by it. The teacher also benefited greatly with the quiet refreshment she received from her class's napping and was able to teach with more joy and excellence.

---

2 If you would like an excellent guide for the napping needs of toddlers, please refer to this article from WebMD at http://www.webmd.com/parenting/features/no-nonsense-napping-guide-for-toddlers #1

I can still remember when I was in kindergarten. After lunch we would go directly to the cubby that had our nap-mats and each of us would pull out our mat (mats we were required to bring from home). We would lay them in a circle and lie upon them. The teacher would then read aloud the next chapter in a book that she had been reading to us. Each day, I looked forward to hearing what would happen next in the continuing book. After a chapter was read, the lights went out and soft music was played. We were not allowed to talk. Sometimes she would forgo the reading out loud, and we would listen to a story tape. Of course, sometimes I never heard the end of the tape because I had fallen fast asleep. No child had an option. None of the children had the option of taking a nap or of getting off their mats. And yes, it was called "nap time."

So how did I get my six-year-old, five-year-old, four-year-old, three-year-old, and one-year-old to nap at the same time while all sharing the same room? I started when they were born, and they did not have a choice. The kids never knew any differently. What they knew was every day after lunch it was time for a nap. When they got older this "nap time" became "reading time." It was a time of refreshment for everyone (especially me).

When the kids were around five or six their bodies did not require as much sleep. They would get on their beds with a few books, or depending on their reading level, a chapter book, and read. Oh, I definitely went through many, many times of different children's coming out to me after about fifteen minutes saying they had napped, or a child asking me if since they had finished their books, could they please "stay up." My answer was generally, "No." I had learned how important this time was for everyone involved. It was important for some to sleep and for some to learn how to be quiet and appreciate books on their own.

The sleep marks on the face and rumpled condition of the hair was a dead giveaway as to whether or not they had actually fallen asleep. If my child had slept, they would come out, find me, and sit down next to me in a groggy state while their bodies started to awaken. Some of my children did not need as much sleep and would sometimes come out with self-induced rumpled hair and fake yawns and say they had slept. What they didn't understand is that hardly any time had passed, and it was obvious they hadn't slept. I would send them back into their rooms, warn them of being quiet, and tell them I would come and get them when nap time was over.

Nap time was never a choice. With the many different children I had, I definitely saw how some of my kids desperately needed a nap all the way up to age five, and how some of my children didn't need that extra amount of sleep past the age of four. All of them, however, needed some quiet time every day.

Do not buy into the new thinking that if your child has a nap, he won't fall asleep at night. Many factors contribute to a child's not falling asleep at night, and I have listed a few.

1. If a child is given a snack right before they go to bed, their body has to work on digesting that food. An occasional dessert or snack is understandable, but making a habit of eating again after dinner is not necessary, and if you get rid of this habit, your children will fall asleep much faster.

2. If your children are not getting enough exercise and fresh air, they won't be able to fall asleep as quickly. Exercise and

fresh air are crucial for the wellbeing of your children and their development. Get some outside toys and let them play. If you do not have an area where they can safely play outside, take them to the park. Like naps, children's playing outside is becoming a thing of the past, and this is ruining their health. Gone are the days when neighborhood children played games like kick the can and capture the flag, when they built forts all day, making roads and cities with trucks and cars, or simply played make believe. Bring this back for your children. It will do them good.

3. Playing video games is another reason your children will not sleep; they are over stimulated. Turn off the games before they go to bed. Allow their minds to settle down. Television can also be affecting how quickly they fall asleep. Turn it all off long before they go to bed and you will notice a big difference.

Many studies have been done to show how important it is to limit children's screen times. This new[2] millennial generation of children will be affected by the ever-increasing technological world. All of the ways in which they will be negatively and positively affected is not yet known because not enough years have passed for long-term studies. However, studies already show screen stimulation experienced often in children is not good for the development of their minds.

I had a conversation with a little boy the other day I hadn't seen for a long time. The things he told me made me very sad for him. He is going into sixth grade and extremely overweight (not the normal pudginess most preteen children experience), and he bragged about how he stays up all night playing video games. It is sad enough when the kids play all day—but all night? I encouraged him to get outside and ride his bike, swim, and catch lizards like his older brothers used to do.

Schedule time for your kids to play outside. I can hear my mother's voice saying, "You kids go outside and play." It was not a punishment. It was a much-needed suggestion (we did not have a choice) for getting some fresh air and using our pent-up energy in creative ways.

Playing outside is not only a good source of vitamin D from the sun and excellent exercise, but it is also good for brains to function as they are actively creating.

We live where the summer months are extremely hot, and I had to be strategic about what time the kids would go outside to play. This was as important to me as eating and sleeping. Fresh air and sunshine is like taking a daily vitamin.

Some days I realized my kids had been inside most of the day, so I would tell them all to go outside for an hour. I did not give them a choice, and sometimes they didn't want to go outside because it was too hot, but before they knew it, hours had passed, and they would have to be called in for dinner.

Remember: you are the parent, and they are the children. You are the overseer of their wellbeing.

Yes, it is easier to give in and let them have something to eat before they go to bed. Yes, it is easier to let them be entertained all evening with videos and movies than it is for them to come up with something to do on their own. Yes, it is easier for them to be inside gaming than it is to make them go outside and play. Nevertheless, children, as well as parents, thrive under being on a good schedule of eating, sleeping, fresh air and exercise.

I will stress something to you as a mom parenting young children... *it is okay for you to schedule your children.* You know better than they do what is good for them. You want what is best for your child.

My typical, daily schedule for ages four and under:

7:00   wake up

7:30   breakfast

7:45   get "ready" for the day (wash face, brush hair, get dressed, make bed, do chores, etc.)

8:30   play

9:30   outside play (I would do yard work during this time and sometimes I would have them help.)

10:30 snack

11:00 movie or play

12:00 lunch

12:30 get ready for nap (pick books and go potty). Yes, this would sometimes take thirty minutes with all of my kids.

1:00   nap

3:00   wake up

3:15   snack

3:30   play, play, play, or watch a movie

6:00   dinner

6:30   hang around

7:30   get ready for bed

8:00   hang out in the living room (we frequently have devotions)

8:20   potty and water

8:30   bed

I have to add here we are a very busy family, so many days we were away from home at least some portion of the day. I did, however, schedule most things around naptime, so appointments and shopping were done before or after naps. We also entertain a lot and having people over also revolved around naptime.

I think parents sometimes need to hear, in their own voices, the absurdity behind the words, "My child won't take a nap," or "My child won't_____" when the child is only two or three years old.

You don't give your children choices about other things in their lives. What is your reason for giving them choices in some areas, especially when you really want them to do the opposite? Think about the things you do not give your children choices about. You make your children wear clothes to the store; you make your children come into the house at night; you strap your children in car seats; you make your children get in the car and go with you so they won't be left alone; you make your children stay off of the roof; you make your children hold your hand when necessary.... Why do you make them do some things and not others? Most of the time you make your children do things because you want them to be safe. You think it is important to be the parent in these situations; therefore, you "make" your children obey.

Does God play a part in our decision-making with our children? Do we only go to Him for help with the "big" issues? Or, do we go to God for everything concerning our precious children? I know God is interested in every part of our parenting, even food or bedtimes. God is interested in how, when, and why our kids are doing what they do.

Although I have given much of this chapter to taking naps, scheduling has many other important components. When your children are on a food schedule, the hundreds of whining scenarios you have experienced of your kids wanting a snack or the whining of false hunger will disappear. Having a regular snack time allows your child to know they won't have to ask for food and they will not have to go hungry.

I don't think in our day and age many kids know the sensation of having their stomachs growl, but hearing it growl is a good thing. Being hungry at snack time, just like being hungry at mealtime, also alleviates a lot of whining and complaining about what is being served.

We recently had a large group of people over, including many little children. I served a simple dinner of taco salad, apple slices, and cookies. One of the children complained about the salad even though he was not tall enough to look on the counter and into the large bowl to see what the salad looked like. He did eat the salad, some apples and three cookies (for someone that young, two would have been plenty). I then heard the mom tell this five-year-old that he could have something else to eat when he got home since he didn't really like the salad.

They left at 8:00 p.m. That meant that after a full meal and much stimulation, he was going to go home and start eating again. What a shame! That little body has had enough and is ready for bed. By the time they get home it will be close to 8:30 p.m., and then after getting ready for bed it will be 9:00 p.m. It will be time for him to go to sleep—not time for another meal. That mom is allowing him to dictate what is best, even though she knows what is best for her child. That is why she is the parent, and he is not.

We all know how good we feel when we have had a good night's rest, eaten a healthy diet, had some exercise, and enjoyed some fresh air. We also know how gross we feel when we have had hardly any sleep, eaten a bunch of junk food, and had little exercise. Your children need you to provide them with all of these things; they won't provide them for themselves.

If you are a harried mom and need a rest, I suggest getting on a schedule. Both you and your child will thrive under the consistency and rest that a schedule brings. Believe in God's assignment for you as the parent and trust you are the parent for a reason. Nurture your child through the structure of a schedule which includes good sleep, sunshine, nutritious food, and exercise. It takes some work, consistency, and discipline on the part of the parent to make this happen, but you will not regret this hard work. The outcome is so rewarding.

Scheduling should not control your life, but being as consistent as possible will help your child be secure and content in life. Nothing trumps the joy of happy children whose parents decide what is best for them.

Chapter 12

Make the Most of Every Car Ride

Are your children in charge of what happens in the car? Do they determine whether or not you have the radio on or what music you listen to? Do they determine how loudly you listen to your music because they are trying to hear their own music or movie?

Train your children when they are little to understand that you, as the parent, will set the pace for what is going on in the car. Training while in the car is not meant to be rigid, for unexpected things can and do happen. Nevertheless, great teaching and learning can happen in the car.

Although my children are older, "car time" is still one of my useful parenting tools. Before you read any farther into this chapter, estimate how much time each week you are in the car with your children. It is important to use that time wisely. It is precious, uninterrupted, parenting time, and the benefits are more valuable than you can imagine.

Before any teaching can be done, however, all electronics must be banned from use during car rides. This is a simple rule, but not always so easy to enforce. With little ones who don't have their own devices, this is quite easy. It takes some self-control from you to not put something in their hands to play with or watch.

As our kids grew older and had their own electronics and phones, we incorporated a rule that if we were in the car for more than an hour, they could have earbuds in or be on any of their devices. Any amount of time less than an hour was spent looking out the window, sometimes listening to the radio, and sometimes having good old conversations.

Here are some examples of teaching and training your young children while you are conversing in the car:

"Don't forget when we get to the Smith's house to be respectful. What are some ways we can be respectful?" Listen to what your kids have to say and then give them some of your own input.

"Remember, we're going to be in somebody else's home. Show them respect by not going into any room you have not been invited to go into, and do not open drawers or take things that are not yours."

"We are almost to Target. Today while we are shopping, I would like for you to help Mommy. I have a lot of things to buy so I will be reading many labels and looking at a lot of prices. It will be helpful to me if today you don't talk to Mommy a lot while we're shopping."

"Remember today when we go to Walmart, Mommy will not be buying anything extra. So, when we get in the store, I want you to remember not to ask Mommy for extra things. I am going to buy only what is on my list. One of the things on my list is_____. If you see that when we're walking around, make sure you tell Mommy so I don't forget to buy it." (Assigning a distraction is helpful, and reminding your child of this distraction as you walk around is fun for your child. Make sure you slow down when you spot it so he has a chance to point it out to you.)

"We are almost at the park; do you remember some of the rules of playing at the park?"

"We are almost at school. I hope you have a good day today in kindergarten. What do you think you will be doing today?"

"When we get to Ashley's wedding, we will be seeing many fancy, pretty things. This will be so exciting; I can't wait to see what she looks like in her dress. I know the wedding will be beautiful because so many people have worked really, really hard to make it beautiful. I want us to be very careful that we take good care of all the beautiful things. Also, I want to remind you kids this is a super special time for Ashley and her new husband, and they are going to be saying things today that will change their lives forever. So, we need to be very quiet and listen very carefully to what is being said. I want you guys to see if the pastor says anything about their being married. I know the pastor will probably tell them at the end they can kiss each other."

"Don't forget when you go to Duke's house to say 'please' if you would like something, to say 'thank you' if you are given something, and to look at his mom or dad if they are speaking to you. Remember their ears are way up high, and your mouth is way below their ears; so you will need to look up, speak clearly, and speak loudly enough for them to hear when you are talking to them."

"I wonder how many old people will be here today? Sometimes old people have a really hard time carrying their plates to the table, so be careful as you walk around and please don't run inside. Wouldn't that be sad if _____ dropped their plate?"

"I can't wait to see Grandma and Grandpa. They always have such yummy food and dessert. I wonder what they will have today. Remember, Grandpa will be watching the ballgame, and he doesn't like for it to be loud inside during the game. Are you going to quietly watch some of the ballgame with Grandpa or go outside and play? Oh, and don't forget Grandma does not want you to play with the sword inside. What does Grandma allow you to do inside?"

Giving your child reminders of how to behave in a store or in someone's home ahead of time can ward off most behavior disasters.

When you are on the way home, recognize any good behavior you saw in your children. Having a discussion immediately following whatever the event may have been is just as beneficial as the warnings ahead of time. Use their fresh memories to cement a particular manner, and they will remember the next time to do it better, or to do it the same. Encourage them in any good behavior they had.

Many hours are spent in the car, and it is the perfect training field for little ones. If your children are always distracted with electronics in the car, you are wasting many hours of their lives when they are a captive audience for training and teaching. Not to mention, some of the most hilarious conversations with little ones take place in the car. You don't want to miss out!

Chapter 13

The Importance of Being on Time

God cares about how we use the time he has given us. One of the ways we can teach our children to use their God-given time wisely is to teach them to be punctual. Understanding that our time is not our own is key. Little children will not understand this when they are young, but they will soon start to understand how precious every moment is.

If you are late to an event, class, appointment, or any other scheduled activity, you affect a lot of people. Stop right now and think about how being late affects other people at an event. Taking a class for instance, some of the effects on others might be: the teacher gets less time to cover the subject; the teacher has to repeat to you what has already been said; all of the students have to listen to everything being repeated; the teacher loses a crucial moment or a train of thought as you enter and "get settled," other students pay attention to your coming in and no longer pay attention to the teacher; therefore, the teacher has to acquire the attention of the class all over again. In another instance, you may have to walk in front of many people to get to your seat, and since other people may have paid (movies, church, concert, play, class) for the instruction or entertainment, in reality you have stolen another person's time and money.

An entire office staff may have to stay late after their work day is done because you came late, and they were kind enough to let you keep your appointment.

Knowing how many people are affected when a person chooses to be late, and how the root of that choice is selfishness, enables you to train your children about the importance of being on time. The godly character trait of thinking about others more than yourself can be instilled when you train your children to be on time.

Oftentimes you may be allowing your child to determine whether you arrive somewhere on time. You might not even know you need to take back your parental authority in this area. You are simply going with the flow, and as soon as everyone seems ready, you head toward the door. Who is deciding whether or not you will be on time? Who is teaching whom the importance of being on time?

> "Look carefully then how you walk, not as unwise but as wise, making the best use of the time, because the days are evil" (Ephesians 5:15-16 ESV).

What interests me is some people consider punctuality to be a personality trait or a character trait, and not simply a choice.

"Oh, she's just an 'on-time' person," they say. Some people's actions, therefore, have put them in a personality category of either having an "on-time" personality or "not-on-time" personality. Some people go through life with this tag and assume it cannot be changed, or they don't care to change it.

I have three friends who are late to everything. I have had multiple conversations with all of them, giving tips to help them be on time. (All three of these friends do not have any children they are getting ready.) Two of these friends set their clocks way ahead so they will not be late; they are still late. I can say "late to everything" because it is not an exaggeration. Well okay... in the month of January, after New Year's resolutions have been made, each friend might arrive on time on a few occasions to something. So that I do not put these friends in a bad light, I would like to add they are disciplined in many other areas of their lives in which I am not disciplined.

A person either plans to be on time or is late. Neither is by chance. This might be my opinion, but if a person chooses to be punctual by planning ahead, then a person also chooses to be late by not planning ahead.

I grew up in a family where we did not dare arrive late; neither did we dare *not* be ready on time. One of my habitually late friends has asked me, "What would've happened to you if you were late?" My answer to her was, "I really don't know." I guess I had enough fear of my father not to be late; however, I don't know what that punishment would have been. I can still hear quite clearly my dad saying, "We are leaving at _____. In. The. Car!" Believe you me, I was in the car at the appointed time. (I want to add that although my father was strict, he was never abusive, and his love for me was evident and sure.)

Because of my training while growing up, it is hard for me to understand why being on time for some people is so difficult. My children still joke with me about how we are early to every event, and if we didn't want to get there early, we had to plan ahead. I use the word training loosely in reference to my upbringing because we were never verbally trained in this area; it was a decision on the part of my parents that we would be on time to everything. It was instilled in us being "on time" was a decision.

A common frustration among mothers is getting somewhere on time with children in tow. What does it take for a mom to be on time? Some of you may not want to hear this and some of you may be glad that the answer is simple. It works flawlessly 99.9% of the time.

Being on time is a decision!

Being on time is a decision—I will be on time!

Before you can be on time, you must first understand that you have made decisions in the past to be late. I know it is truly not as easy as it sounds, because it is one more thing in your life requiring discipline and consistency. And we all know being disciplined is hard. Being on time takes planning ahead and leaving your house *much* earlier than you think you need to leave. Being on time takes determination, and eliminating frustrations is the key.

Most habitually late people leave their house with the exact amount of driving time it takes to pull into the parking lot of their destination. This is not enough time, however, to be on time for your event or appointment. It is only enough time to be in the parking lot. If it takes twenty minutes to get somewhere, do not leave your house twenty minutes ahead of time and expect to arrive at the appointment on time. Twenty minutes might be enough time to be pulling into a parking lot, but it is not enough time to actually be where you are supposed to be at the appointed time.

From an early age our kids started working for many of the people in our community doing yard work, mechanics, gardening, cleaning, babysitting, recycling, and whatever odd thing the person wanted them to do. One of the men that hired our boys had a motto:

Being early is on time
Being on time is late
Being late is unacceptable!

He did not want the kids he employed to be pulling into the parking area or riding in (bikes and motorcycles) at the time they were supposed to be there. They still had to park or get off their bikes, take off helmets, get out working gear and water bottles, etc., and then be given instructions. He wanted them ready to work at the appointed time. It seemed like all of the teen boys in our area grew up and went off to college at the same time, so this man started to hire the boys' sisters. The sisters were all warned by their brothers about this motto.

The average time it takes loading up all of your kids with the things needed for an errand or event, getting buckled in car seats, and starting your car and driving off takes more than a couple of minutes. Arriving at your destination, finding a parking space, parking your car, gathering your purse and belongings, getting your children out of their car seats, wiping a face, changing an unexpected dirty diaper, walking through the parking lot, going into the building, using the restroom with all of your kids, washing hands, and more... takes more than just a couple of minutes. And, on top of all that, many of you must account for traffic. (Not me! When my dad was out visiting, he used to joke that if we saw another car at a stop sign, it must be rush hour.) Allowing *a lot* of extra time for all of these things enables you to arrive on time with a smile on your face.

Planning ahead for your next appointment can make the drive stress-free and enjoyable. Put anything you can in the car the night before. Put addresses to locations in your phone or purse so you are not trying to do this while driving. Have an idea of where you are going ahead of time. If it is a familiar destination, still leave extra time for the unexpected.

I am in the habit of taking a drink with me wherever I go. (We live in the desert, and it can be crucial during the summer.) I know trying to carry everything out to the car in the morning can be overwhelming. I am also notorious for spilling things (coffee every time I am wearing white... you would think I would learn my lesson) as I lean into the car, so it is best if I put the majority of my things in the car the night before, so that when I am actually walking out to the car, I only have to make one trip, and my arms are not overloaded.

I put these things in my car ahead of time: library books (yes, I still use the library), donations, store returns, kids' sports gear, presents for the occasion, dry cleaning, and mail. Putting these things in the car ahead of time makes going out the next day easier, and it saves me time not having to make several trips to the car when I am trying to be on time. I started this habit many years ago because it is much easier to put things in the car when the kids are in bed, rather than trying to get it all in the car while scrambling to get kids into car seats, along with the massive amount of stuff that goes along with going places with toddlers.

You have the same twenty-four hours in your day on-time people have. Plan ahead to be on time. It might take awhile for you to apply new behaviors and for them to become a habit, but do not lose heart—you are teaching the next generation that being on time is a selfless act of kindness, and being on time positively affects a lot of people.

Chapter 14

Work Hard! Finish Well!

When a child learns to stay at a task, do the task well, and finish the job, the rest of his life is positively affected. If you want to know exactly how important it is to teach your child these things when they are young, hire a few pre-teen or teenage kids to do some work for you. I am often the leader of such a group, and the kids who can actually be given a task, do the job without looking at their phones or stopping to rest every couple of minutes, and completely finish the job (pick up remaining trash, put tools away, leave the area looking finished) are few and far between.

Are you a harried mom because you are overwhelmed with how much there is to do around the house? Have you tried to get your kids to help, and it is futile? Are you teaching your children how to be responsible and work hard so they can someday keep a job, provide for their families, and take care of their own homes? Or have they trained you to do it all on your own? It might sound strange to say the children have done some training in this area, but that is the truth. If you have not trained them to start working, then they are simply training you to do it all on your own.

A friend of mine has a five-year-old boy. She has given him the chore of cleaning the cat's litter box. She was a bit frustrated the other day because she had a long battle with him to get him to do it. And then when it was all said and done, he didn't do the job the way his mother wanted it done. Remember, he is only five and has just finished kindergarten.

This question has been asked of me many times: "How do you get your kids to do their chores?" The answer is—start when they are little. When you start something when they are small, it is so much easier because that activity becomes "normal" to them. This is not to say that there were not times when one of our children did not do their chores or did not do them well. But on the whole, they did their chores because that is what our family does in the morning. A mother's tone of voice and presentation of commands is extremely important (I know mine wasn't always perfect). Giving commands without threats or rewards is the key. You want your child, when they are little, to obey simply because they have been told to do something.

Taking the cat's litter box as an example, inform the child a week ahead of time, every day, because he is growing up to be such a big boy he *gets* to have a big-boy chore. In this way, he will anticipate being given a responsibility that comes with age. Show him how to do it (using a light-hearted voice—remember, you do not want them to dread it), make him aware of the fact it takes very little time to complete the chore, and tell him you expect him to do it well. After you explain it all, put the litter back and tell him in a fun voice, "Now it is your turn. Let Mama see you try it."

It doesn't have to be perfect, but tell your child sometimes you will check his job and call him back to do it again if you think it wasn't done well the first time. This allows him to know he will have times of correction when given a chore, and he will not be disappointed or defensive when you give him correction on completing it. Sometimes if he consistently lacks doing his chore or not doing it as specified, then a punishment is needed. Make it clear and simple and enforce it consistently.

You are the parent and you can come up with the punishment that works. If your punishment is not working, then you need to find one that does.

We live in a one-story, five-bedroom house. It is not a large house because each of the rooms is quite small, but it suits our family well. Years ago, the workload of our constantly growing family started to overwhelm me, but I realized how much of the workload could be taken off my own shoulders and dispersed among my children. Not only would it alleviate some of my work, but it would also teach them many godly characteristics that would one day benefit them in their own future families.

- I wanted my children to help with the mundane things when they were younger and with the bigger things when they got older. So, chores were started. At the beginning of their kindergarten school year, our children were given chores.

- Months ahead of time, and in some instances even years, I would "brainwash" them into thinking that chores were an exciting privilege that comes with age.

I would say things like:

"In just one year you get to do chores."

"In two months, you will be old enough to have a chore."

"Wow! You are such a big helper. Pretty soon you will be doing chores."

"Our house looks so nice because everyone is helping with chores."

"When you are bigger, you will be strong enough to use a chain-saw like Daddy."

"Pretty soon you will be as big as your brother and be able to push the wheelbarrow."

Our children looked forward to receiving their first chores. They did not get rewarded for doing these tasks or given an allowance. Allowances were not something that our budget allowed, and we wanted our children to learn everyone in the family participated in the upkeep of the home.

Early in the morning, while my husband is getting for work, I:

— start laundry
— get dressed
— make my bed
— get mail ready to go out
— fix my husband's breakfast (Not a big deal. He eats two pieces of toast with peanut butter and jelly on them almost every day—his choice.)

— empty the dishwasher (unless it was someone's chore)

— empty the dish-drying rack if something dried overnight

— change diapers

— feed baby

— water my plants

Because I am always very busy doing "chores" in the morning, this seemed an appropriate time for the kids to be doing their chores as well. Kids seem to work better if they don't feel like they are the only ones working.

It is also important you are up and around during chore time to make sure all is getting done. When everyone is working, no one seems to mind (not much anyway).

It did help for our kids to know we had friends who owned a dairy, and their three boys had to get up before 5:00 a.m. to help feed the cows. My kids also had many friends who had to do chores before they went to school and after they came home. Also, when I read to my kids, it became a habit to point out things in books I wanted them to glean about a good work ethic.

If the house in the book looked nice, I might randomly say, "Wow! They must do a lot of chores around their house."

If a bed was made well, I might say something like, "That bed is made so well. Do you think their mom helped them, or do you think they did it all on their own?"

If the child or adult in the book was working, I might draw attention to it by saying, "They probably learned how to do _____ from working around the house or working for a neighbor." I even added things that would appear to have actually happened in the story to get my kids' brains engaged in thinking about the positive results of hard work.

After reading a book, children's brains are still engaged in the story. That is why it is important to read things to your children you want them to think about or emulate. I also pointed out positive working behaviors to my small children during and after they watched a movie. In a nonchalant way, direct your children's thinking to the positive results of hard work. It can be very random, such as, "Wow! Look at his room. I wonder if he picks it up in the morning or at night."

"They have a huge yard. I wonder how long it took the family to rake all of that."

Just throwing brain teasers into your children's mind puts their little minds on wanting to do a good job.

Because we assigned two to three chores to our children starting at a young age, and because we have seven children, it was sometimes hard to come up with enough chores for everyone. It was important enough to us, however, that our children learn while they were little how to accomplish more than one task well, so I actually had to drum up some chores for the little ones. We started with simple chores and increased the difficulty as they grew older. Some of the simple things I would give our four or five-year-olds were: picking up the couch pillows and throw blankets off the living room floor, straightening the rug by the door or in the hallway, turning off the night light in the hallway, making sure that nothing was under the kitchen couch, or taking the dusting wand and simply swishing it under a desk near our front door (dust bunnies accumulated daily and could be seen very easily as one walked down the hallway). We heat our house with wood, and collecting kindling was an excellent thing for even a three-year-old to do. Giving them a bucket and telling them to fill it with sticks was a great chore for our small children. (Yes, we do have central heat, and occasionally we use it. But we do live in the desert and prefer a wood stove to heat our house. Plus, it saves money.)

The most important thing is the training and not the specific chores your children do. You want them to be able to:

— do their chores without being asked

— do their chores exactly how they were told or shown

— do their chores in a specified time-frame

— do their chores with a good attitude

— do their chores without complaining

As they grow older, the jobs get harder; but by the time your child is seven, they will have already done thousands of chores with a good attitude and finished them well, enabling them to accomplish, in a timely manner, the more difficult chores as they grow older.

Continue to use brainteasers to engage your child's thinking to want to do their work well. These thought-provokers should be said, or pointed out to them, all throughout the week. For instance: When you pull up to the store that looks nice on the outside, say, "I wonder whose job it is to clean up the sidewalks out here? They sure do a good job." Usually people only notice a parking lot or the front of the store when the trash cans are overflowing, shopping carts are all over the place, or fast food is spilled, but we want to engage our children's minds to think about jobs being well-done, and that somebody is doing good work even when given the gross jobs.

Point out a clean restroom to your children. Point out the fact that there was toilet paper in the stall, and you are glad that somebody was doing their job. This is positive training, and training outside of when they are actually doing their chores works wonders. It is better to point out positive jobs well-done you want your small children to copy rather than negative work you don't want them to copy.

Get your little ones excited about working by making positive comments about future chores.

"In a couple of years, you will be old enough to get the 'dog chore' or 'take out the trash.'"

"You sweep the sidewalk so well that pretty soon you'll get to empty the ash bucket."

"You are getting so tall, you are almost big enough for the _____chore."

This verbalizing allows them to look forward to greater responsibility and not dread it.

It is important to give them praise and thanks if they do their jobs well. As I type this, I realize it has been a long time since I have praised my own kids for the chores they are doing. I will do that today!

Some of the chores we give to our older children are:

— take out the recycling

— feed the dogs

— feed the chickens or take food scraps to them (when they were still alive)

— net and brush the pool

— wipe the bathroom sink and counter

— sweep the porch and sidewalk

— clean up the lawn

— empty the dishwasher

— empty the ash bucket

Making their beds was not a chore—it was understood!

Each child was given two tasks to do in the morning—one hard and one easy. On Saturdays, each one had a little extra, such as cleaning the chicken pen, picking up dog doo, adding chlorine to the pool, taking buckets to the burn pile, shaking out rugs, and emptying the shoe bucket.

Chores only took about five to ten minutes a day, sometimes quite a bit less. Multiply that times seven and it totals approximately five hours of work each week—work I would be doing on my own if each child was not expected to contribute as part of the family.

Because I homeschool, my kids are home for lunch every day. Years ago, I also started having the kids do one lunch chore. These chores revolve around lunch and only take a few minutes. Everyone is doing chores at the same time, the chores are simple, and the habit of doing lunch chores had been set in place years before, so no one minds—well almost never minds.

Our lunch chores are:

— gather trash from all rooms and put into the dumpster outside

— clear and wipe the table

— sweep the kitchen floor

— bring in laundry from the clothesline (Almost every day, except Sundays, I hung out two loads of laundry, but with my kids growing up and moving away, it has dwindled quite a bit.)

Watering plants and trees outside is the worst job because it takes longer than five minutes, but we all take turns, so it is not so bad. Some of what is growing on our property is on automatic timers and some things have to be watered by hand, but the most precious thing of all is our small circle of grass. Not many people can get grass to grow out here in the desert—it is a precious commodity, especially to those of us who are from back East.

When there was a baby, entertaining the baby for a few minutes until the kitchen was cleaned up was a favorite chore.

Think of things you do every day. Make a list, starting with the most difficult, and assign those things for your kids to do.

Do not make it a big deal when assigning chores to your children. Simply state what is expected and then make sure it is done. When everyone is cleaning up after a meal, and doing chores at the same time, no one seems to mind. It is done so habitually it becomes second nature.

One of the things I did when it came to assigning chores was to have each child keep their chores for long periods of time (three to six months). This allows each child to get used to doing that particular chore and to learn how to do it well. Assigning chores for long periods of time also helped me remember who was doing what chore. Sometimes I would notice a chore wasn't done well, and I needed to correct the child; and sometimes I would notice a chore done exceptionally well, and I needed to praise him. The difficulty of the chores changed according to the seasons and weather, so switching enabled the chores to be more evenly distributed among them.

Many people have asked me over the years, "How do you make your kids do their chores?"

- Start young.
- Do not cajole them.
- Give chores and instructions matter-of-factly.
- Show them how to do it.
- Work at the same time.
- Give a time frame.
- Give praise and correction. (I should have given a lot more praise and a little less correction.)

We started when our children were young, so punishment for undone chores was rarely needed. On occasion, however, I gave an extra job if their chores were not done well or not finished on time.

Chores are not something our kids do because they are home-schooled. Having chores teaches them how to be hard workers, to be of good character, to have a good work ethic, to be respectful of property, and to help keep the house nice and enjoyable for all who live there and for those who come into our home.

When our children wake up in the morning, they are expected to get dressed, make their beds, do their chores, and then eat.

Because we live in the desert, chores were done mostly in the morning because of triple digit weather in the afternoon. When everyone does about ten minutes of work each day, a lot gets done.

Now that I have adult children who no longer live at home, I can confirm from their feedback that having daily chores was a good thing.

The wind blows constantly here, and dusting needs to be done often. I started a tradition when the kids were two and three years old, of putting our Benny and Joon soundtrack into the CD player when it was time to dust. Then I would give each of my children a couple of damp paper towels. I would then give them a piece of "dusting energy." This "energy" was always candy. (Even after twenty years, no one dusts our furniture before the expected dusting energy.)

Each child was assigned several pieces of furniture, and with music blaring, the dusting began. As the kids got older and taller, they were given rags with oil for the furniture and told how to avoid getting oil on the glass, lamp shades, etc. Since many of the kids are grown and gone, we don't listen to Benny and Joon as much anymore, but when it is time to dust, the kids still say, "We need energy." Having my smallest ones help was great because my toddlers were more capable of dusting the legs of the furniture than I was.

Unfortunately, I loved the Benny and Joon soundtrack, and now I cannot listen to it without thinking that I need to dust.

When it comes to chores and teaching your children to work, do not think they are being worked too hard. People don't generally look back with regrets over having worked hard but, in general, tend to brag about the hard work they did. When they are adults, they are usually very grateful that they were taught how to work when they were children.

Teaching your children to work hard and finish well is good for them and for you.

Chapter 15

Teach Your Child to Swim

Does your child know how to swim? If he or she does not, is your child in charge of whether or not they learn to swim? It is interesting to me to observe when a parent gives their child the choice.

I do not have a biblical principle for teaching your child to swim, but I do think it is important enough to include a chapter about it.

For years I worked as a lifeguard at a summer camp. At the beginning of each week, we had a new group of campers. These campers had to take the swim test before they could swim in the lake. Every year I was amazed at the number of teenagers who had never learned to swim. I was even more amazed at the number of counselors who could not swim. The two most common reasons given for not knowing how to swim are:

"We don't have anywhere to swim."

"My mom doesn't know how to swim, so I never learned."

When I was growing up, I just assumed everyone learned how to swim when they were little in the same way they learned how to ride a bike. When I was in high school, the home in which I lived had a pool, and I don't remember anyone ever coming over who didn't know how to swim. Therefore, I went into adult life assuming that the majority of people knew how to swim. Not until I started living in my current home—with a swimming pool—did I realize how many adults can't swim.

It seems we have almost as many adults come to our home who can't swim as those who can. A parent who cannot swim can hand down to her children her great fear of water. Therefore, I like to encourage people to come and swim, especially if they have children. I cannot stress enough—teach your children to swim at a young age. Find a lake or some other source of deeper water, take advantage of the hospitality of someone who has a pool, or check with your local community center to see if they provide any sort of swimming lessons.

Teach your children to swim!

Why do I think this is such a big deal? When a person does not know how to swim, it not only affects their own lives but the lives of those around them. I have seen it firsthand. Swimming affects:

— attending certain parties, events, birthday parties

— your marriage (if one spouse loves water activities and the other can't swim)

— where you choose employment (possibly passing up an awesome opportunity because of your lack of swimming ability)

— babysitting or childcare—life or death in a possible drowning situation

— school activities (field trips, electives, etc.)

— friendships

— self-confidence

— travel, lodging, vacations

— summer camp for your children

You might say you don't have accessibility to swimming, but is that the truth or just an excuse?

A child does not need formal lessons to become a proficient swimmer. By proficient, I mean a person who can jump into deep water, come up, catch a breath, and confidently swim to shallow water. Your child doesn't need formal swimming lessons (although these are great), nor does your child need to swim like an Olympian; all you need to do is find a pool, lake, pond, river, community center, or neighbor, and let your children swim. It is certainly a wise investment of your time for them to learn to swim.

Although I have seen many children have a great fear of swimming because their moms cannot swim, I have also seen parents who don't know how to swim be determined that their children not go through life in the same way they have. They expose them to as many swimming opportunities as possible.

Because some parents have a huge fear of the water, they don't want to "make" their kids get in the water.

I have seen moms who don't want their hair to get wet, or don't want to wear a bathing suit in public, so it is inconvenient for that to be a "good" day to learn to swim. It might be the only occasion for their kids to learn to swim, and they are not taking advantage of the opportunity.

The benefits of your children learning to swim are invaluable. Here are some suggestions for teaching them to swim.

Do:

— take advantage of every opportunity they have to swim

— get in the water with your children

— show them how to get their faces wet

— show them how to go under water

— take advantage of family members who swim

— teach them to blow bubbles

— teach them to kick both in and out of the water

Don't:

— stay out of the water

— chat with your friends on the sidelines

— cajole them to want to swim

— be afraid to ruin your hair or makeup

— belittle them

— let them plug their nose (they need both arms to learn)

If you can't swim, take someone with you who can show them how to get wet.

Swimming is carried on from generation to generation. If you can't swim, don't let that be carried on—break the cycle and allow your kids to learn to swim.

Clear your calendar in the summer, and save money for lessons if finances are a factor.

Not being a confident swimmer will affect your children's lives in so many areas, and their learning is up to you as a parent. Give them this ability, joy, talent, exercise, purpose, and positive experience.

Not only will the ability to swim affect your children's lives, but it will affect many others as well. You have no idea how many times your children will have the opportunity to swim or not swim, but it is up to you to see that they are prepared when opportunities arise. Your children may have to pass up many positive things throughout their lives just because they never learned to swim. And one more thing… moms… if you can swim but do not feel confident, then follow all the above advice and do what you can to increase your own swimming confidence and ability. It will change your life.

Teach your children to swim!

Chapter 16

Learn to Respect Others and Their Property

What does respect mean anymore? The dictionary defines respect as esteem for another, a sense of the worth or excellence of a person, or admiration for a personal quality or ability of another, treating another with proper acceptance or courtesy, such as for the elderly. The Bible also speaks about respect: "In everything, therefore, treat people the same way you want them to treat you..." (Matthew 7:12 NASB).

Last week I saw an old friend I hadn't seen for about a year. I was amazed at how much her youngest girl had grown. She looked to be about eight-years-old, but I found out she was only five. My friend's daughter was tucking herself closely into her mother's skirt because of her shyness.

Trying to get a better look at her, I addressed this little girl by name and asked her how old she was. She did not look up, but she did answer me. I was surprised that I got an answer from a girl as shy as she.

The mom, without missing a beat, used her daughter's name and said, "Remember to look at someone when you are talking to them."

The little girl looked right up into my face and repeated her answer of five, and then looked back down because she was done talking to me.

She did this so quickly and had such a pleasant expression on her face it was really quite wonderful to see. The mother had instructed her child matter-of-factly; although she used a gentle voice, she expected obedience.

It was a rare and beautiful exchange I wish all moms with young children could have witnessed. This is called respect. The little girl had already learned to respect and obey her mother and was being taught to respect others.

Does God want us to choose whom we respect? I think we are to respect all people, for they are made in the image of God.

It is interesting, as I write many of these chapters, how convicted I am in my own life. Are my children learning to be respectful of others by the way I teach them? Are they seeing and hearing respect come from me?

Respect touches so many of the areas in which we are teaching our children. Find as many ways as possible, in your everyday life, to teach your children how to respect others.

Here are a few examples:

Teach your children to put things back where they belong so that someone else doesn't have to do it for them. Give your children reasons why they are being told to do certain things and steer their thinking to put other people first. You might want them to pick up because you want a clean house. This will not compute with your children sometimes, because usually small children do not usually care if the house is clean. But if you can steer their thinking to clean up after themselves because of respect for other people, it will give them a purpose for what they are doing and a reason for them to do it in the future.

Teach your child not to litter. Explain to them that someone will have to pick up the trash, and how nice it would be if that person had just a little bit less trash to have to pick up that day. Talk about the other person with your child. Explain that they may have had a bad morning, or they may have had a sad thing happen in their life. By not leaving extra trash for them to pick up, it might help them have a better day.

Teach your children to look at people when they are being spoken to or when someone speaks to them. It is a simple command and can be learned. (This training takes place at home as you remind them to look at you when they are being spoken to or when they are speaking to you.)

Teach your child not to enter a room making noise. Give them different scenarios of things possibly taking place in that room. Even if the person in that room might not appear to be busy or care if there is sudden noise, they don't know that before entering; therefore, they need to be respectful. You want to engage your kid's minds to be thinking about other people.

While writing this chapter, I asked my husband what he wished small children would learn. At the moment, he was sitting on the bench underneath our kitchen window, looking out over our property. He answered, "I wish kids were taught to respect people's property." As I have mentioned before in my book, we often have people over, and the most of them have children. Some of these children respect our things, and some do not.

Teach your children to respect other people's things. This does not come naturally to most; it needs to be taught. Explaining to your kids how to treat things before you get to another person's house is crucial. Talk about anything you think your child will be using or any areas that they might be going into. Explain what is acceptable and what is not. Teach your children about where to go and where not to go. Explain to them obvious off-limit areas and why. Tell your children several things that are okay to do and several things that are not. Teach these things at home and reinforce in the car before you arrive. Respecting another person's property should be taught over and over again.

Teach your children to respect God's creation. I have seen children kill animals just for the sake of killing or stomp wildlife just for the fun of stomping. When they are taught that God's creation is amazing and beautiful, respect for His creation will follow. I encourage you to talk often about God's creation so your children will develop a respect for it.

Teach your children respect for authority. Start this while they are still young. What your children hear you say about people in leadership and authority over you is how your children are learning to respect the authority in their own lives. It is that simple! How you speak of those in leadership and authority in your own life is teaching your children how to respond to the authority in their lives.

What do your children hear you say about:

— your pastor

— their teacher

— your teacher

— their coach

— policemen

— the president

— your boss

— your husband's boss

— your parents

— your husband's parents

— the leader of an event

Oh, the dangers of your children overhearing your disrespect of other people. Your children are not missing anything you say, so fill their little ears with words of respect and honor for the people in your life, and they will learn to respect and honor people in their lives. (I still need to work on this.) Remember: everyone has faults and is full of sin, so don't wait for another person's perfection and good behavior to merit your respect. The Bible is very clear about the things we say.

> But no one can tame the tongue; it is a restless evil and full of deadly poison. With it we bless our Lord and Father, and with it we curse men, who have been made in the likeness of God; from the same mouth come both blessing and cursing. My brethren, these things ought not to be this way. Does a fountain send out from the same opening both fresh and bitter water? (James 3:8-11 NASB)

Give respect now. Give it to all.

Chapter 17

Give Your Child Guided Choices

A good way to understand this principle is through the scenario of giving a small child a choice of kid-friendly cereal. A parent opens the cupboard and may say to his child, "Would you like Lucky Charms or Cap'n Crunch?" Most children that age love those cereals, but with the cupboards open, their eyes immediately scan the cupboard contents. Before they even know what the other options are, they say, "No! I want those."

Most of the time, not even knowing what they are pointing at, they just know you have made a choice for them. Because you have trained them *not to accept your choices,* they put themselves in charge and demand something different than you suggest. You don't think it is a big deal... it is just cereal. No big deal! Right? *Wrong!*

My husband and I took a parenting class when we had several small children. This class was enjoyable because we were not allowed to take our children, and we were both required to attend. Date Night! It meant we could pay attention, learn together, and be on the same page about parenting. So, we got a babysitter once a week and went to the leader's house to learn, socialize, and have refreshments. We looked forward to this because it was a nice break from our children, and we got to socialize with other parents at the same phase in their lives as we were.

One of the things we learned is giving children a choice with designated guidelines is a good thing. They like to choose things on their own, but most of the time they want to be in charge and make choices without boundaries. It is important while your small children are making choices, they still understand who the authority is, and who is in charge.

For instance: it is time for your two-year-old to get dressed, and you have chosen her outfit for the day. The drawer, however, is still open, but the shorts and shirt you have pulled out of the drawer are ready for her to put on. A typical scenario might be when your child spots her favorite purple butterfly shirt at the top of the drawer, and sees you did not get it out for her to wear. She says in a nice voice, "I want to wear my purple butterfly shirt." You pull the butterfly shirt out and say in a singsong voice, "Okay! Now let's get you dressed."

Even without saying anything, you had told her by getting out her outfit you had decided what you wanted her to wear. Your child simply usurped your authority and took charge. Is there anything wrong with her wearing her purple butterfly shirt? No. The problem is you had already chosen what she was going to wear, and she knew it, and she used her own way of being in charge to get what she wanted.

Now we will play out this scenario in a way your child can still have choices but at the same time learn to obey God-given authority structure. Until your child is an adult, he or she will be under your authority and living with choices within guidelines. Of course, those guidelines are expanding all the time as they get older, but when they are small, the boundaries need to be small. Two-year-olds have no reason to be in charge of what clothes they have, where their clothes are purchased, how they get their clothes (such as hand-me-downs), when they put their clothes on, and what clothes they put on. Nevertheless, we do want to train them to make good choices within boundaries.

Starting fresh, inform your two-year-old (or whatever age your child may be) that from now on they get to choose what they are going to wear on some days, and Mommy is going to choose what they wear on the other days. Before they start looking at their choices, remind them of this.

One of the things my husband and I gleaned from the parenting class was to allow our children to have choices—but with guidelines. For instance, it is time for your three-year-old to get dressed. In the previous year, if your child has had the undisciplined privilege of choosing his or her own clothes, you probably have some training to do.

It is morning and you tell your child it is time to get dressed. You have already placed her clothes out on the bed for her to put on. The shirt you picked out and put on the bed is a shirt with two dogs on the front. When she comes into the room, she discovers to her horror you have picked out the dog shirt instead of the princess shirt. She insists she wants to wear her princess shirt. Several thoughts go through your mind in a split-second—it is just a shirt; it is no big deal. You proceed to get out the princess shirt. You don't want to get in a battle with her on a nice morning. Her princess shirt is not clean, but you guess it's not *that* dirty. You can get it out of the hamper. You think to yourself, "I should hide that shirt. Maybe, I can talk her into this dog shirt."

Even if your daughter asked in the nicest way to wear her princess shirt, it is vital in a situation like this you win this battle. Why is this important? Little scenarios like this occur all day long, all week long. You are teaching her you are the parent, you are the authority figure, and she is not in charge of herself. God has set up authority in her life, and she needs to obey that authority.

Little situations like this are the best training for your small children. They need to understand following authority is a good thing, and their choices are a good thing within the guidelines of authority. They will always have authority, guidelines, and choices. Train our children to know how to live with all three of these things in a good way.

You may decide to get out two outfits for your child and let them choose which one they want to wear. You may decide to get out three shirts and let them choose which one they want to wear. It can be amusing to watch children. You might want to get out five shirts, leave the drawer open, and just see if they go for one of the five shirts you have given them to choose among, or if they are eyeing the drawer to make their own decisions. You may open the drawer for them and tell them to choose anything they want to, but you have opened the drawer, and you have given them permission to do that. It is important you set the guidelines for their choices.

It might be breakfast time and you have pulled out Lucky Charms and milk and are starting to pour them into a bowl. Your child says, "May I please have Life this morning?" Well, he did ask nicely. He did say please. You did buy Life for him to eat. Life is just as good for him as Lucky Charms. He is going to eat both at some point anyway. And you don't feel like dealing with the battle, so you proceed to get out the Life. Who was in charge? Who is running breakfast time in your home? It is very important that you deal with the battle and that you win it. Inform him that on some mornings he will have a choice, and some mornings he will not. It is that simple.

You might want to tell him the next morning he will not have a choice, but on Friday he will. Keep it simple. Keep your voice jovial and be consistent. You might want to give him three choices one morning among a bagel, a pop tart, or toast. Even with three choices he might say he wants yogurt. It is crucial he learns how to respond to authority and stay within guidelines. Set these guidelines at a young age so he understands the authority in his life. We all have to respond to authority throughout our lives.

Plan ahead and decide you are the parent in every situation. Plan some choices that you are going to give your child, and plan times when he will not have a choice. He will quickly learn he is not in charge, but you are. He will thrive under consistent, loving structure.

If you are wondering how your child is doing in this area, pick up two books and have a few extra books visible to your child. Start to read. If your child has a good handle on respecting authority, he will settle in and listen to the book that is being read. If you have some work to do, your child will start squirming to get down to see what his other choices are among the books. The same goes for page turning.

Sometimes parents do not want to give guidelines because they want their children to have the freedom to explore or to express themselves. They can express themselves and explore thousands of ways without undermining their parents' authority.

Children may not always have choices. All day long, every day, there are numerous situations you can use as a training ground for teaching them the godly chain of authority. Sometimes you will give them a choice, and sometimes you will not.

Start today: inside or outside, milk or juice, movies, entertainment, bath time, brushing teeth, nap time, toys, shoes, socks, colors—choices, choices, choices all day long.

Your affirmative action is the key. It is all about voice, words, tenacity, and prayer.

Today I watched a mother try to get her two-year-old to leave the park. She followed him all around, through sprinklers, inside bushes, around cars, uphill, out of sight, all the while telling him it was time to go, and asking him to please come on or they would be late to pick up Daddy. The mother ended up bodily carrying a kicking and screaming child to the car and buckling him in while he was having a fit.

This scenario probably would not have happened if that child had been taught to obey and had learned the boundaries of obedience. Most likely, none of this would have happened if he had been taught Mommy is in charge, of his boundaries, where he goes, and what time they leave the store.

If children do not learn to respect when they are young, their disobedience will turn into bigger problems when they are older.

Train at home.

Train in any little situation you can find, and enjoy taking your children to the park.

Give your children choices within boundaries when they are little so they will make good choices without boundaries when they are adults.

Chapter 18

Teach Your Child to Lose Gracefully

Play a game with your child and win. Have a race with your child and win. Give a prize to one of your children for something and see how your other child responds when they don't get the prize. Does your child know how to lose gracefully?

Losing can be hard. Life can be hard. Why is teaching your child to lose important?

Not learning how to lose well leads to anger, pride, cheating and even depression. These character traits go against the godly character traits we are trying to instill in our children.

Life is full of hardships, losses, and disappointments. God allows this and orchestrates our lives. When children learn, from a young age, how to respond correctly to the losses in life, they will be better prepared as adults when these things happen.

A good way to start exposing them to the uncomfortable feeling of loss and disappointment is to teach them how to lose. The best way to do this is to play games with them. Yes, I think just like learning to win, they need to learn how to lose. Being a good loser takes self-control and respect for others.

I am not saying you have to sit down and play a board game with your child every day. That is not a bad idea, but because we are speaking of small children, the games can be short. If you see your child is a bad loser, then you might:

Teach your child how to say, "Good job," to the winner at the end of a game and how to say, "Bummer, I could have played better. Let's play again so I can try a little harder."

Whatever it may take, help them through the process of losing. As a teacher of young children, I can see in my experiences and observations of "bad losers," that it takes practice to be a good loser. Usually after they have been in my class long enough, they all know how to lose. And after they learn how to lose well, I make sure I "rig" a game so they get to experience winning as well. I like to praise them when they win... and when they lose.

In all of the different venues in which I teach children, I have noticed well-behaved children are good losers. What do I mean by this? The children who are well-behaved during all aspects of the class are the same children who respond well to losing a game.

We play a few games on a regular basis:

Mother May I?: When it is the child's turn to move forward, if he forgets to say "Mother may I," he has to go all the way back to the start. Some children go all the way back immediately when told. Some of them go back and drop to the floor and pout. Some of them try to cheat by not going all the way back.

The children who go all the way back are also the ones who line up well, sit quietly during the lesson, raise their hands before speaking, and eat their snacks without a lot of drama.

Red Light/Green Light: In this game when the word "red light" is spoken from the leader, all children must stop immediately. The goal is to reach the end mark during a green light. If a child does not stop immediately when "red light" is spoken, he has to go all the way back to the start.

It is the same children who do not go back to the start with a good attitude, and it is the same ones who try to cheat by inching their way up, or saying, "No, I stopped." Sometimes when I send them back, they might drop to the floor, say they don't want to play anymore, and stubbornly pout.

On the other hand, many children enjoy the game, follow the rules, and understand there is only one winner, and it might not be them.

Hot Potato and Musical Chairs are two games that quickly teach a child how to lose. If the potato lands on them or they don't sit in a chair when the music stops, they are out. It is somewhat interesting to watch the kids respond. Some of them respond well to loss and disappointment, and some do not. Teach your children how to respond well to losing when they are little.

Life is full of trials and tribulations, losses and disappointments. However, life is also full of joy and celebration, peace and contentment. Understanding God orchestrates it all is something we continue to learn and experience throughout our lives. Teach your children to properly deal with life's circumstances.

I don't know all of the psychological reasoning behind the fact that the well-behaved kids are also the good losers, but if you think your child needs to work on losing, start playing a lot of short games with him and don't let him win. Do not worry about his quitting. He will try and try again to beat you because he wants to spend time with you, but what you say each time the game is over is important.

If your child is on a team, be careful what you say when their team has a loss. It is important that your child understands the other team won because maybe they simply played a better game. Say this out loud to your kids. This is not in place of encouraging your children by praising them for their good efforts and pointing out something they did well during the game.

Most kids want a reason for losing so they look good in spite of their loss. Some parents might blame it on the referee. Some parents might blame it on the other team, the field, the ball, the equipment, the weather, a teammate, etc. It is pathetic at times to listen at the end of children's games to hear why a child thinks they lost. And it is even more pathetic to hear the reasons parents give their children for the loss. Teach your children you will always have winners and losers, and it is okay to be either one.

As well as winning and losing a game, there is also the art of participation. This takes some training as well. Although I am not going to devote an entire chapter on this, I think it would do parents well to observe how well their child participates in something where they are expected to participate, even though it might not be something they like to do.

Again, the children who participate well are the same ones who behave well during the rest of class time. Why is it that some kids naturally sit still, participate in everything, and line up in an orderly fashion? They have been taught. Is your child one of these children? Are you waiting until your child is in kindergarten for a teacher to train them in these areas? Do not waste any more precious time in your child's life. You teach them and teach them now while they are young.

God allows all kinds of things to take place in our lives, and putting God in the picture of a win *or* a loss is key. The sooner your children realize God is in control of their lives, the sooner they will progress toward becoming adults with godly character.

> Yours, O Lord, is the greatness and the power and the glory and the victory and the majesty, for all that is in the heavens and in the earth is yours. Yours is the kingdom, O LORD, and you are exalted as head above all. Both riches and honor come from you, and you rule over all. In your hand are power and might, and in your hand it is to make great and to give strength to all (1 Chronicles 29:11-12 ESV).

Chapter 19

Ridiculous Things Mothers Say

Mothers say many things to their children on a regular basis, and that is perfectly natural. There are at least five things mothers say that are ridiculous.

1. "Let's not...."

"Let's" implies that you are including yourself in the wrong doing. You are not doing the offense, so do not use the word let's or let us. It is more effective to use the child's name and then give the correction.

2. "One, two.... Don't make me say three."

What is going to happen when you get to three? Would the same thing happen if you were consistent and you chose not to count to three? Will your child actually experience some sort of discipline when you get to three? Make the discipline happen before you start counting. For instance: What if you say, "Billy, get down off that ladder," and he does not get down? You discipline him right then in the same way you would have disciplined him if you had reached the number three when counting.

Children have learned to obey according to how you have trained them to obey. If you state what they are to do clearly, and you expect obedience or else there will be a punishment. They will learn to obey when the command is first given.

If you train your child to know that when you give them a command they don't have to obey until you get to the number three, and only then do they get a punishment for disobedience, they will learn to wait until number three to obey. Your children soon learn and know you do not intend to punish them after counting to three, so you have trained disobedience to them through your idle threats. Make it easy on your future and on your child's future. When giving a command, use their name at the beginning of the command, make the command clear, and follow through with whatever discipline you have decided for the disobedience. It only takes a few times of giving a clear command and the expectation of immediate obedience for your child to start obeying immediately on a consistent basis.

3. "Did you hear what I said?"

Have you trained your children not to obey because they have not *actually heard* you give them a command? I was in a grocery store aisle the other day and heard an obviously harassed mother tell her child to stay close by her side. The boy was walking back and forth across the aisle studying items on the shelves. The mother raised her voice a little and repeated her original instruction. He continued walking back and forth across the aisle. At that point, she raised her voice another level, but this time she called him by his first, middle and last name: "John Mark Doe, did you hear me?" With a sweet smile on his face, he turned to his mother and said,

"Did you call me, Mama?" She had trained her child *not to hear her* unless the volume was at a certain level, and he was called by his full name. What are you training your child to hear?

4. "Okay?"

Ending instruction with the word "okay" implies you are asking for their permission. You are not asking them to sanction the instruction that is being given, so do not ask them if they are okay with it. It is fine for you to ask them if they understand (if they are old enough to understand), but do not ask them if it is okay. They are not the parent, and a toddler should not be setting the guidelines for the home.

5. "Do you want a spanking?"

This is a ridiculous thing to say. Need I say more?

In the Bible, God does not use the words let's, when referencing our offenses. Neither does God sugarcoat commands. His commands are clear, as well as the consequences of disobeying them or rewards for obeying them. The Bible gives sufficient evidence of people's failing to obey God and being punished to prove He means what He says.

Chapter 20

Teach Your Child to Obey

Not only do we want our children to be compassionate servants, but we also want them to be obedient. I cannot tell you how many times I have witnessed blatant disrespect, temper tantrums, and selfish battles going on between a mother and a toddler. I try not to stare, but it truly amazes me. Is the child raising the mother, or is the mother raising the child?

Before reading this chapter, I want you to know that administering pain with correction is so effective that when done with consistency, love and not anger, the result will be: no fits of rage from your child, no public tantrums (or tantrums at home for that matter), seldom a repeat of the same bad behavior, the end to your giving false threats, and the end to horrific shopping trips with your little ones. Administering pain with correction will make for pleasant shopping experiences, obedient children, and calm, cool, and collected parents. Understand I want to be candid with you, so... please continue with caution and an open mind.

Last week I was at our local outlet mall where we have an abundance of foreign travelers. I was waiting in line to make my purchase, and a little boy behind me said something to his father. His father answered him, and then the boy kicked him right in the shin. He appeared to be about three years old, but because he spoke in a foreign language, I do not know what the father had said to him that merited such a response. The father then repeated what he said, and he repeated the kick! I venture to guess that kick was not the first time he had acted in such a manner.

In the Old Testament, hundreds of verses are written about God's instructing the Israelites to hear his teachings and to fear Him. In addition to telling the adults how to live, the book of Deuteronomy instructed them over and over to teach their children at home, all day, everything they had learned about God: "Recite them to your children and talk about them when you are at home and when you are away, when you lie down and when you rise" (Deuteronomy 6:7 NRSV).

The Bible commands us to *train* our children, and in my opinion, the majority of this training must take place at home. When this happens, public displays of bad behavior are few and far between.

I imagine you are wondering what I would have done in the kicking situation. Personally, I never had a kicking situation, but I would have pushed my cart to the side, excused myself from the line, and with child in tow gone out to the car. While at the car, I would have given my child a spanking. Then I would have gone back in the store and finished my shopping.

Several times over the course of raising my children, a situation required me to wheel my grocery cart into the store's cooler so that my groceries would not get warm, and take care of "training" my child out in the car. This was usually if I had to tell my children to stop doing something more than once. Maybe they were touching too many things, or stepping up onto the cart (sometimes I allowed this—it depended on how many kids were with me, how heavy the cart was or how crowded the store was), or maybe they were bugging their siblings, etc. Sometimes many things went on among my kids while I was shopping that were not a big deal, but other times if I made a specific command, then I expected immediate obedience. Of course, when one received a spanking, it was remembered for a long time by all. That is the beauty of not giving false threats. If you command immediate obedience, then you deal with just a fraction of troublesome recurrences of the same offense in the future.

We have all been in a store and heard parents giving ridiculous reasoning, empty threats, name calling, counting to three, cajoling, and yanking their children, with the hope their children will miraculously change their behavior. Baffling!

The other day I observed the following scenario: a mother was trying to keep an approximately two-year-old child in the stroller while the child was screaming, crying and yanking his body all about.

The mom said in a voice that could be heard above her child's tantrum, "Hang on, Honey. Let Mommy just finish one more thing, and then we will get a Starbucks."

The child did not stop.

What amazed me the most was the fact that the mother was frantically hurrying her shopping for the child to get his Starbucks. What would have happened if she had not hurried? Not only was

I amazed at the compliance of this mother to her toddler, but I was also amazed that this child knew what Starbucks was. This is backwards training. A child should be trained to obey his mother, not the mother trained to obey the child.

In a situation like this, I caution you not to start something that could become an expected habit. Train your children to be able to shop without getting a reward. This might mean that you will have to train yourself to shop without buying yourself a reward as well.

Again, you might be wondering what I would do if my child acted in this way. Bending down close to my child's ear, I would clearly tell him to stop screaming and sit straight or we were going to go out to the car for a spanking. I would say it once, say it clearly, and follow through. If he did not obey immediately, I would push my cart out of the way and take him outside. After his spanking, I would go back into the store and finish my shopping. If you have a stubborn child, be prepared to go out to the car more than once.

I believe it is extremely important to give yourself extra time shopping if you have small children with you. Having plenty of time helps you to be consistent, patient, and unflustered. Do not be in too much of a hurry or training your children will take second place, and shopping will become more important than raising well-behaved, godly children. Plan ahead so your priorities are in the right order.

It can be embarrassing to take your children out of a situation in front of people, but, believe me, strangers are glad to see you "take care of" tantrums and disrespect.

Part of the strategy of peaceful shopping is planning for the war zone. I say this tongue-in-cheek, but shopping with toddlers often appears to be the front-line of the war zone. Planning for the battle can be done in the car. Explain to your child what you are shopping for, how difficult it can be to find things, read labels, compare prices, etc. Giving creative things to think in the store can be a wonderful distraction. I used to ask my children how many people they thought we would see that we knew. This put their minds on something fun and off having to be patient while Mommy shopped. Do not underestimate how much they comprehend. Their minds are extraordinary.

Use car time wisely. Between errands, have a discussion (training session) with your children. For instance, tell them how you expect them to behave in the next store and discuss how people were behaving in the last store, pointing out good behavior. Allow them to talk about what behavior they observed. Make up some funny scenarios depicting bad behavior and good behavior. Perhaps ask them what would happen if the cashier started to cry and threw himself on the floor, or if the cashier stopped what he was doing to grab a pack of gum from the shelf and then begged you to buy it. Ask them why they think a particular child acted in a certain way. Not only are these discussions educational, but they can be a lot of fun. Discussing behavior, whether bad or good, enables your children to reflect on what happened, and helps them to determine in their hearts their behavior will be good in the next store.

Warning: discussing other's behavior for training purposes is good, but discussing the behavior of children whom you know can be gossip; therefore, use caution when discussing people you know.

Although car training is tremendously effective, I cannot emphasize enough the importance of training your children at home. Consistent training at home will alleviate 99% of the need to discipline in public. It will be worth it in the long run, and it will be a joy to take your toddlers out in public. You might be amazed at how many people compliment your children's behavior in the future.

Try not to habitually reward good behavior with tangible things. Every once in a while is okay, but you want your children to be satisfied with verbal praise and not to expect something just for behaving in a good way. If their behavior was exceptional because of a long wait, or other unforeseen events, rewards are wonderful, but we want our children to learn to behave well even if there is no reward given.

Last week I went to IKEA; and if you have ever been to IKEA, you are familiar with the arrows on the floor that directing people through the entire store in an orderly fashion. This is a well-thought-out plan to make customers have to walk by everything in the whole store before they can exit. The floor plan of the store is so well-done and pleasing to the eye that strolling through each section of the store is a delight.

About halfway through the maze of arrows, I heard a child's cry. At first, I thought it was possibly high-pitched laughing, but when it didn't stop, my curiosity got the best of me. As I joined the crowd of onlookers, it became obvious it was a tantrum. Some of the crowd may have been fooled, but not me. I am a mother, and we mothers know the difference among cries—newborn, hurting, tantrum, fake, or sad cries—and we know them well.

After what seemed like way too long, the mother picked up her child and started to follow the arrows out of the store. I wish I knew the end of the story. I do know, however, what I would have done in this situation. I would have trained my children at home so that this kind of situation would not have happened in public.

By the time a child is four years old, he will experience hundreds of situations where staying in a seated position is crucial for his own safety. Your child does not need to understand safety, but does need to obey the instruction of staying seated.

Because we live in the desert with poisonous sidewinder rattlesnakes, I want my child to hear the word "stop" and to obey right away. Sometimes immediate obedience is crucial for the safety of your child; other times immediate obedience is just for the sanity of the parent.

Consistent training at home will alleviate 99 % of the need to discipline in public.

Understanding the purpose of administering punishment that hurts is vital. If done correctly, the parent should be able to give their child a command, in a normal voice, and the child will obey right away. This kind of training is done when the child is preschool age; and all they need to understand is that you are their loving parent, and when you tell them to do something, they should do it.

When my firstborn son was about two, he was fascinated with a hideous black desert bug called a stink bug. I am including the scientific name of the bug so that you can look it up before you read on [pinacate beetle USA desert stink bug]. These bugs are about an inch long and raise their rear ends to let off a stinky scent when they feel danger approaching. They are also very slow. Time and time again I would catch my son with one in his hand looking closely at it. I knew his wheels were turning and wanted to know what they tasted like.

The first time I saw his mouth open wide and his little hand about to drop it in, I freaked out! I had to stop him more than once from putting one of those disgusting bugs in his mouth. But when they were prevalent, I did not want to have to keep a hawk eye on him every second we were outside. So, I finally decided I needed to spank him if he picked up one of these bugs again. I made it clear and I spanked his hand rather hard the next time he picked one up, and that solved my problem. As he got a little bit older, I could let him pick them up, but I used firm instruction for him not to put them in his mouth. Along with my restriction, I used a happy voice and bent down and watched them or scooted them with a stick, so he understood he could play with them as long as he did not pick them up. Obedience is what I wanted, not to stifle his creativity and desire to explore. Believe me... my kids had plenty of discovery time with critters in the desert. Young kids understand clear direction.

I have witnessed hundreds of scenarios in which small children must be cajoled or threatened into doing the simplest of tasks, i.e. eating breakfast, getting dressed, brushing teeth, getting into bed, going potty, sitting still, being washed, picking up toys, walking into a store, being quiet, putting on "swimmies," and the list goes on. Most of these tasks happen several times a day, which adds up to more than one hundred altercations a week.

It is sad to see what some parents put themselves through so many times in one week alone, not to mention over a three-year period. When a child understands they are the child and you are in charge, he is so much happier and is not confused in any way. Their little minds can comprehend this simple truth. Later when their minds are more developed, you can start to teach them the whys behind each command. No battles, just happiness.

Jesus was the ultimate example of obedience. He obeyed even though He didn't want to—He obeyed even though it was hard. In the Bible, the Gospel accounts of Jesus's last days reveal just how hard it was for Him to obey. This was evident when after asking His heavenly Father if it were possible not to have to die, an angel gave Him strength, and when He continued to pray in earnest, his sweat was like drops of blood. He was then flogged, spat upon, tormented, and finally crucified.

Luke 22:39-23:49

Jesus went out as usual to the Mount of Olives, and his disciples followed him. On reaching the place, he said to them, "Pray that you will not fall into temptation." He withdrew about a stone's throw beyond them, knelt down and prayed, "Father, if you are willing, take this cup from me; yet not my will, but yours be done." An angel from heaven appeared to him and strengthened him. And being in anguish, he prayed more earnestly, and his sweat was like drops of blood falling to the ground.

When he rose from prayer and went back to the disciples, he found them asleep, exhausted from sorrow. "Why are you sleeping?" he asked them. "Get up and pray so that you will not fall into temptation."

While he was still speaking a crowd came up, and the man who was called Judas, one of the Twelve, was leading them. He approached Jesus to kiss him, but Jesus asked him, "Judas, are you betraying the Son of Man with a kiss?"

When Jesus' followers saw what was going to happen, they said, "Lord, should we strike with our swords?" And one of them struck the servant of the high priest, cutting off his right ear.

But Jesus answered, "No more of this!" And he touched the man's ear and healed him.

Then Jesus said to the chief priests, the officers of the temple guard, and the elders, who had come for him, "Am I leading a rebellion, that you have come with swords and clubs? Every day I was with you in the temple courts, and you did not lay a hand on me. But this is your hour—when darkness reigns."

Then seizing him, they led him away and took him into the house of the high priest. Peter followed at a distance. And when some there had kindled a fire in the middle of the courtyard and had sat down together, Peter sat down with them. A servant girl saw him seated there in the firelight. She looked closely at him and said, "This man was with him."

But he denied it. "Woman, I don't know him," he said.

A little later someone else saw him and said, "You also are one of them."

"Man, I am not!" Peter replied.

About an hour later another asserted, "Certainly this fellow was with him, for he is a Galilean."

Peter replied, "Man, I don't know what you're talking about!" Just as he was speaking, the rooster crowed. The Lord turned and looked straight at Peter. Then Peter remembered the word the Lord had spoken to him: "Before the rooster crows today, you will disown me three times." And he went outside and wept bitterly.

The men who were guarding Jesus began mocking and beating him. They blindfolded him and demanded, "Prophesy! Who hit you?" And they said many other insulting things to him.

At daybreak the council of the elders of the people, both the chief priests and the teachers of the law, met together, and Jesus was led before them. "If you are the Messiah," they said, "tell us."

Jesus answered, "If I tell you, you will not believe me, and if I asked you, you would not answer. But from now on, the Son of Man will be seated at the right hand of the mighty God."

They all asked, "Are you then the Son of God?"

He replied, "You say that I am."

Then they said, "Why do we need any more testimony? We have heard it from his own lips."

Then the whole assembly rose and led him off to Pilate. And they began to accuse him, saying, "We have found this man subverting our nation. He opposes payment of taxes to Caesar and claims to be Messiah, a king."

So Pilate asked Jesus, "Are you the king of the Jews?"

"You have said so," Jesus replied.

Then Pilate announced to the chief priests and the crowd, "I find no basis for a charge against this man."

But they insisted, "He stirs up the people all over Judea by his teaching. He started in Galilee and has come all the way here."

On hearing this, Pilate asked if the man was a Galilean. When he learned that Jesus was under Herod's jurisdiction, he sent him to Herod, who was also in Jerusalem at that time.

When Herod saw Jesus, he was greatly pleased, because for a long time he had been wanting to see him. From what he had heard about him, he hoped to see him perform a sign of some sort. He plied him with many questions, but Jesus gave him no answer. The chief priests and the teachers of the law were standing there, vehemently accusing him. Then Herod and his soldiers ridiculed and mocked him. Dressing him in an elegant robe, they sent him back to Pilate. That day Herod and Pilate became friends—before this they had been enemies.

Pilate called together the chief priests, the rulers and the people, and said to them, "You brought me this man as one who was inciting the people to rebellion. I have examined him in your presence and have found no basis for your charges against him. Neither has Herod, for he sent him back to us; as you can see, he has done nothing to deserve death. Therefore, I will punish him and then release him."

But the whole crowd shouted, "Away with this man! Release Barabbas to us!" (Barabbas had been thrown into prison for an insurrection in the city, and for murder.)

Wanting to release Jesus, Pilate appealed to them again. But they kept shouting, "Crucify him! Crucify him!"

For the third time he spoke to them: "Why? What crime has this man committed? I have found in him no grounds for the death penalty. Therefore I will have him punished and then release him."

But with loud shouts they insistently demanded that he be crucified, and their shouts prevailed. So Pilate decided to grant their demand. He released the man who had been thrown into prison for insurrection and murder, the one they asked for, and surrendered Jesus to their will.

As the soldiers led him away, they seized Simon from Cyrene, who was on his way in from the country, and put the cross on him and made him carry it behind Jesus. A large number of people followed him, including women who mourned and wailed for him. Jesus turned and said to them, "Daughters of Jerusalem, do not weep for me; weep for yourselves and for your children. For the time will come when you will say, 'Blessed are the childless women, the wombs that never bore and the breasts that never nursed!' Then 'they will say to the mountains, "Fall on us!" and to the hills, "Cover us!"'

For if people do these things when the tree is green, what will happen when it is dry?"

Two other men, both criminals, were also led out with him to be executed. When they came to the place called the Skull, they crucified him there, along with the criminals—one on his right, the other on his left. Jesus said, "Father, forgive them, for they do not know what they are doing." And they divided up his clothes by casting lots.

The people stood watching, and the rulers even sneered at him. They said, "He saved others; let him save himself if he is God's Messiah, the Chosen One."

The soldiers also came up and mocked him. They offered him wine vinegar and said, "If you are the king of the Jews, save yourself."

There was a written notice above him, which read: this is the king of the jews.

One of the criminals who hung there hurled insults at him: "Aren't you the Messiah? Save yourself and us!"

But the other criminal rebuked him. "Don't you fear God," he said, "since you are under the same sentence? We are punished justly, for we are getting what our deeds deserve. But this man has done nothing wrong."

Then he said, "Jesus, remember me when you come into your kingdom."

Jesus answered him, "Truly I tell you, today you will be with me in paradise."

It was now about noon, and darkness came over the whole land until three in the afternoon, for the sun stopped shining. And the curtain of the temple was torn in two. Jesus called out with a loud voice, "Father, into your hands I commit my spirit." When he had said this, he breathed his last.

The centurion, seeing what had happened, praised God and said, "Surely this was a righteous man." When all the people who had gathered to witness this sight saw what took place, they beat their breasts and went away. But all those who knew him, including the women who had followed him from Galilee, stood at a distance, watching these things.

Christ was the ultimate example of obedience.

Obedience in children is a beautiful thing. It was so encouraging to me as a mom to have people tell me how wonderful it was to see obedient children. My children were many times not obedient, but it sure was worth the hard work it took when they were.

Spanking as a Means of Discipline

Spanking is not fashionable today. As a matter of fact, parents today might not even want to admit they spank their children. A few years after my husband and I were first married, we had a couple of small children, and we took a Christian parenting course. This course talked about the benefits of spanking, from a Christian perspective. We were already spanking our children, but this gave us the encouragement we needed to continue.

I don't think a course like that would be well-attended in 2017. As a matter of fact, a couple of my friends encouraged me not to put spanking in my book for fear it would turn readers away. I did not feel like I could leave it out since it played such a vital part in our parenting.

One of the things my husband reminded me of that we had learned in our parenting course was giving our children enough attention, love and physical touch. If they don't get enough attention, love and physical touch away from spanking times, they might resort to being naughty for the attention that a spanking gives them. Give your children plenty of attention and love when they are being good.

My husband and I strongly believe God gives clear instructions in the Bible for using pain as an instrument for correction and training. The following verses show what God thinks about a parent inflicting pain while correcting his or her children.

"Whoever spares the rod hates his son, but he who loves him is diligent to discipline him" (Proverbs 13:24 ESV).

"Discipline your son, for there is hope; do not set your heart on putting him to death" (Proverbs 19:18 ESV).

"Foolishness is bound in the heart of a child; but the rod of correction shall drive it far from him" (Proverbs 22:15 KJV).

"Do not withhold discipline from a child; if you strike him with a rod, he will not die. If you strike him with the rod, you will save his soul from Sheol [death]" (Proverbs 23:13-14 ESV).

"The rod and reproof give wisdom: but a child left to himself bringeth his mother to shame" (Proverbs 29:15 KJV).

"Fathers, do not provoke your children to anger, but bring them up in the discipline and instruction of the Lord" (Ephesians 6:4 ESV).

As believers, we understand the "instruction of the Lord" is the whole Word of God.

I have heard many parents say that spanking doesn't work for their children. I personally belive the reason their spankings don't work is they have a different definition of the word "spanking."

In our home, we had several key components to a spanking:

Spanking was a session; it took time. (Because we had so many little ones, I often felt like I was spanking all the time.)

Spanking was done in private.

Spanking was not done with our hands, but with a small paddle my husband made. (He actually made two of these paddles so we could have one in the car.)

The spanking hurt—tears should be present.

The spanking was done on the child's bottom.

Discussion of the offense was included, and more discussion as their understanding increased.

Praying, hugging, and saying, "I love you," was included at the end.

When the spanking was over—the situation was over. Good moods for all! I would like to say this was always the case, but it wasn't.

It is crucial that you start when your child is young.

Our children received the most spankings from ages two through four. By the time our children were five or six, the spankings became fewer and farther between. As they got older, we used many different forms of discipline or punishment that "fit the crime" better.

We are not perfect parents, and we did not always have perfect spanking sessions. I am sure our kids could share stories of their imperfect parents, but our love was sure and their regular obedience was a joy.

One time when my oldest son was around eleven or twelve, he had done something wrong. (I can't remember what it was, or I would include it.) I couldn't figure out the right punishment. I wanted to take care of it right away, so I told him he was going to get a spanking. It had been a long, long time since he had received a spanking, and he was a big boy (however, not bigger than I—yet). I knew I had to "give it all I had" for this spanking to hurt.

He bent over, and I gave him about seven really hard swats. I stopped. There was silence and a long pause. He then stood up and turned around. We looked at each other and started laughing. I knew then that his spanking days were over (they actually had been for years). I think the humiliation of being that old and getting spanked was punishment enough. But you know, we had the sweetest talk and mother/son time. To this day we still bring it up occasionally, and he is twenty-four. It is now a fond memory for both of us.

The outcome of consistently spanking your children when they are disobedient, and using spanking for the training and admonition of the Lord, makes for happy, obedient children, and more purposeful parenting.

When consistent, your children will know what is expected of them and what they can expect when they do not obey. One of the keys of spanking is giving clear instructions.

Every time you tell your small children to do something, you should not have to threaten a spanking if they do not obey. For a while, though, when they are little, this might be the most effective.

For instance, if your three-year-old continues to empty her clothes out of the drawers onto the floor, day after day, make it clear if she does it again, she will be spanked. If the spanking is done in love and the spanking hurts, chances are you will not be dealing with her clothes all over the floor again. Sometimes, however, we did have to spank more than once for the same offense.

What I tend to see parents doing is marching into the situation, pulling their child up off the floor, giving him a few swats and saying angrily, "I've told you a thousand times to stop pulling your clothes out of the drawer." The parent then proceeds to put all the clothing back in the drawer (rather than making the child do it), and then carries their child away from the situation.

What worked for us was to get our children's attention, make sure they were looking at us and listening, and then tell them they were not to pull their clothes out of the drawer anymore. Make them put the clothes back (you can help them), and then shut the drawer. Look them in the eye, making sure they are paying attention, and in a calm voice say, "If you take the clothes out of the drawer again, you will get a spanking."

You don't have to be mad, but do be matter-of-fact. Please be very careful not to spank your children when you are angry. This will not be good for either of you.

Nevertheless, be ready—you know, as well as I do, the minute you turn the corner, they are going to pull the clothes out of the drawer again. That's okay! Your child is testing you to see if you are going to do what you say, and they want to know if you are in charge. They are learning to obey, learning Mommy means what she says, and Mommy is in charge—they are not in charge of Mommy. Remember consistency is the key.

Sometimes when I didn't feel like spanking, I had to tell myself it was worth it. The obedience and happiness following a spanking was worth it, and knowing that situation would rarely happen again, also made it worth it. The time it took to spank my child far out-weighed dealing with the same naughtiness over and over, or giving false threats, counting, getting upset, yelling, or having to bodily move my child away from a situation again and again.

If the spanking you give is not going to hurt—don't bother; it won't do any good.

After a situation like the clothing and the drawer, try to find interesting ways to make your child want to improve. For instance, find pictures in books or magazines where things are neatly put away. Point it out without making reference to the previous mess or spanking. If you see your child looking at another child, and that child looks neat and tidy, say to him, "I really like that blue skirt on Tiffany. I wonder if she hangs that in her closet or if she folds it up and puts it in her drawer?"

Giving our kids things to think about in reference to what they are learning is ideal, positive reinforcement. You could say something like, "I sure am glad Daddy doesn't take all of his clothes out of his drawer and throw them on the floor after I have folded them and put them away. He likes it when I fold his clothes, because it is easier for him to get ready for work."

Little things that get your children's minds working after a spanking are helpful in making them not want to do the same offense again. Remember they are so little and our words are useful.

I need to add here as a foster parent we are not allowed to spank our foster children, and I am sure there are some sufficient replacements for spanking. We are fostering babies only, so spanking does not apply in our caregiving of them.

We as parents are not perfect; we are going to make mistakes. Our children are not perfect; they are going to make mistakes. However, as a believer, we have the perfect Holy Spirit living inside of us, and we have all that we need in His perfect work. Let's pass this along to our children as we instruct them in the wisdom of God's Word, encouraging them to emulate the character of Jesus Christ.

It is interesting to see how irrelevant God's Word becomes as trends change. The world has trained us to look for alternative ways to discipline our children. Are the Scriptures relevant to us today? Spanking used to be a common form of discipline, even in public schools. Did it not work?

Can we rely on what God says in His Word to be a guideline for parenting? Do we believe His Word is sufficient?

Is the Bible timeless, or is it out of fashion?

We are all using something to direct us in our parenting decisions. It is okay to pick up a parenting book and glean from it, or to ask for advice from somebody who seems to be skilled at parenting, but use these things as extras and not as a replacement for the Word of God. The Bible is sufficient.

Chapter 21

Thoughts Come Before Actions

Minds are going all the time. I just recently went to a pumpkin-carving party. I had to enjoy myself as a spectator for the evening because I had recently had foot surgery and was in a wheelchair. Seven children were present, and the oldest child was six. As I sat there taking in all of the festivities, what I enjoyed doing the most was watching the two-year-old boy tootle around.

For two hours he was happy and content in a very small living room and kitchen area. I watched as his eyeballs roamed around for his next adventure. If he spotted shoes, he went straight to the shoes and put them on, even if they were his sister's plastic high heel shoes. He walked onto the kitchen floor and enjoyed listening to them click and clack on the tile until he was done with that fascination.

He then went to the table where the pumpkin carving was taking place and watched there for a little while without getting in the way. When this had filled his fascination, he turned his head and his eyes scanned the room. He walked toward his next fascination—a leftover, uneaten piece of pizza on somebody's paper plate.

He stood and looked at it, contemplating, I'm sure, on whether or not to pick it up and take a bite. After a few seconds, his eyes moved on to the next thing that captured his attention.

His brain was going at all times. I could have taken the opportunity to say twenty or thirty different things that would have caused him to go in a certain direction, pick up a certain toy, or react a certain way. That is how influential planting a thought can be.

When a parent realizes the brain is engaged at all times, he or she will realize how important the spoken word is. I don't mean long, drawn-out conversations, but little tidbits causing the child to think and want to behave in a certain way.

For instance, if you have asked your three-year-old to pick up their toys, be close to them. As they are picking up their toys, be busy doing something along the lines of cleaning up as well.

An important part of sidling up next to your children while they are doing tasks is for you to be working also. Then you can throw in the teaching moments causing them to think and fill their brain with thoughts of good character.

Let me take this a little farther. As your child starts to pick up his scattered Legos, the task might look a bit daunting. As you stay busy putting away clothes, straightening the closet, wiping off the dresser or straightening the bed, you can say little things to him such as:

"Do you think you can pick all those Legos up before I get these clothes put away?"

"Wow! Maybe I should take a picture of your picking up Legos so Grandma can see how well you take care of the presents she gives you."

"I wonder how _____ (name of an old person, a person in a wheelchair, or a person you know who uses crutches, etc.) picks up her things when they are all over the floor. I wonder if she has help. She would have to be really careful to get all of the pieces picked up so that her crutch didn't hit one and cause her to fall, or allow her to get her wheelchair across the floor easily."

Another scenario might involve asking your children to go get ready for bed. Be close at hand but busy doing something else so they can obey on their own. Here are a few things you might say to get their brains going:

"Remember the picture of that boy in the magazine? I wonder if he has pajamas. I wonder how many pairs he has? I wonder if he needs help putting them on, or if he can do it all by himself?"

"I wonder if that little boy in the magazine has a toothbrush. I wonder if they have toothpaste in his country."

"Wow! I sure am glad we have toothbrushes and toothpaste here, because I am glad I have all of my teeth still in my mouth."

Do not ask your children questions during this time; just make statements causing them to think. It causes them to want to do well. If you have any world health or missionary magazines, or publications showing people in dire needs from other countries, show them to your children. This will cause them to ask you good questions, and allow you to have a basis for making statements.

If you want your child to do a good job of taking care of his animal, then while he is at the job of caring for his animal, busy yourself in the same area and start his brain engaging. For instance, you might say, "I wonder if Buster is super hungry when you feed him? I wonder if his stomach growls? He's so lucky you are taking care of him, because I know some dogs don't have very much room to walk around because nobody cleans their area. But Buster has lots of room to play and sleep because you do such a good job of picking up his messes."

Conversations like this should be one-sided and not require answers. You should also have long pauses in between the statements made. You want your children to start thinking about what you have said but be able to continue to work. You want what you have said to cause them to want to do their jobs well and want to do their jobs in the future.

Thoughts come before actions!

The fact you are working while they are working makes the jobs seem more normal to them. It will teach them they are part of the family, and those who live in the home all work together to keep it a well-functioning home.

Maybe your child's job is to set the table or to dry some dishes. This is a time where you could say something like: "It sure is nice putting food on a clean dry plate. Thank you, Emily, for doing your job so well. I sure wouldn't want to put this serving of mashed potatoes on a dirty or wet plate."

This causes them to think about the jobs they have done. You have rewarded them through praise; their brains will continue to engage from that short exhortation and cause them to want to do a good job in the future.

The Bible tells us, "Do not be conformed to this world, but be transformed by the renewal of your mind, that by testing you may discern what is the will of God, what is good and acceptable and perfect" (Romans 12:2 ESV).

Engage your child's brain toward good thoughts. Nothing can become an action if it is not first in the mind. Remember: thoughts come before actions.

Conclusion

I love being a mom, and I love helping younger mothers with encouragement, advice, and babysitting when I can. When the time came we no longer had any babies, my husband and I decided to become certified foster parents. We have been doing foster care for just a few years, and it is way different than I expected, but so far it has been a very good thing for our family.

That being said, doing foster care has put us back in the baby and toddler world, and I am in contact with many moms. I meet moms, foster moms, and caregivers from every imaginable walk of life. This has made me realize, all the more, that making every moment count when your kids are little is crucial in this day and age.

Parenting a child today is done by many different categories of people—two parents, one parent, stepparents, grandma, great grandma, two grandparents, aunts and uncles, great aunt and/or great uncle, one foster parent or two foster parents. Even though children are being raised by someone other than their biological father and mother, they all have the same basic needs. Caregivers need some little tidbits of advice that will help them navigate the oh-so-tiring but oh-so-rewarding path of raising children.

Sometimes in a person's life, hearing one sentence can change their life. Sometimes observing one action and imitating that action can change their life. Sometimes a teacher teaches one new concept, and it changes their student's life. A person might do what may seem the smallest thing for another person, and it changes the recipient's life. It is important not to underestimate how even the smallest details can influence our child's life.

Every child is moldable, trainable, and in need of nurturing. God designed them this way. Bringing children up in the admonition of the Lord, and understanding that parenting every day revolves around the relevancy of God's Word, will result in a new, godly generation. We are not perfect moms; neither are our children perfect, and God knows this. In spite of this, God has given us the capability to raise them in a way that pleases Him.

Looking back over my twenty-five years of parenting, I certainly have some regrets. For instance, I reflect on many times when I was more interested in the dirty sock that was on the floor rather than giving my children my undivided attention. I focused more, at times, on correction instead of encouragement. My children could probably tell countless stories of my faults, and yet I am sure they could also tell countless stories of my strengths. Nevertheless, what I have written in this book are things that helped me through the often-complicated maze of raising small children.

We as parents, grandparents, foster parents, aunts, uncles, and caregivers must not become too comfortable just raising our kids each day the way the world exemplifies parenting. The parenting ways of the world have caused us to think of the Bible as irrelevant, causing worldly parenting to become the norm. Therefore, let us parent differently *from* the world so our children will make a godly difference *in* this world.

It is with great excitement, fear, and humility I have written this book. I hope and pray it brings help to anyone who reads its contents.

BRINGING UP A GODLY CHILD
Hugh Lasater

Raising a child
In this world of sin
Is harder now
Than it's ever been.

So many distractions,
Satan trying to lead them astray,
I fall to my knees
Every day and pray.

Praying that You
Will be true to Your Word,
And if they stray,
They will return.

You tell me to teach them,
And that I will do,
But in the end, Lord,
It's all up to You.

Try as I might
To teach them Your way,
I know full well,
They still may stray.

Your Word is clear,
And I understand;
So I submit them this day
Into Your hands.

Asking for Your
Will to be done
In the lives of
My daughter and son.

Made in the USA
Monee, IL
22 May 2022

96867871R00115